The
COME AWAY
MY BELOVED
Daily Devotional

The
COME AWAY
MY BELOVED
Daily Devotional

Frances J. Roberts

BARBOUR
PUBLISHING

Published by Barbour Publishing, Inc., P.O. Box
719, Uhrichsville, Ohio 44683
www.barbourbooks.com

*Our mission is to publish and distribute
inspirational products offering exceptional value
and biblical encouragement to the masses.*

Member of the
Evangelical Christian
Publishers Association

Printed in China.

Introduction

"Forged in the crucible of life" is how author Frances J. Roberts describes her million-selling book *Come Away My Beloved*, selections of which you'll find throughout this devotional. Excerpts from her other books—*Progress of Another Pilgrim, Dialogues with God, On the Highroad of Surrender,* and *Make Haste My Beloved*—are also included in this first-ever, 365-day compilation of Mrs. Roberts' writings.

The preface to *Come Away My Beloved* applies equally to all of Frances Roberts' works:

In the midst of each day's joys and trials has come the ministering Spirit of the Heavenly Father and the Lord Jesus Christ, bringing words of encouragement, hope, comfort, and conviction.

To gain the maximum blessing from this book, read it carefully and prayerfully, a little at a time, searching always for the special treasure of truth for your own need. He who knows you by name and understands your deepest longings will speak to your heart from these pages, shutting out the world around you and bringing you into fellowship with Himself.

Whether you are just beginning your Christian walk or have grown into a fuller stature in Christ, you will be equally challenged and helped. Some books give instruction for Christian living; others inspire to greater devotion. This book will do both as you open your soul to its living message.

With this book go many prayers that God will enrich every life it touches. Surely we are all bound together in one family in Christ through the bonds of His Holy Spirit.

Each day for an entire year, you'll find a thought-provoking excerpt from one of Frances J. Roberts' books, a relevant scripture, and a question prompting further reflection. Our hope is that, for the next year, *The Come Away My Beloved Daily Devotional* will draw you ever more closely to the Father's heart.

The Master Artist

from *Come Away My Belov*

And God saw every thing that he had made, and,
behold, it was very good.

GENESIS 1:31

I make no idle strokes. What I do is never haphazard. I am never merely mixing colors out of casual curiosity. My every move is one of vital creativity, and every stroke is part of the whole.

Never be dismayed by apparent incongruity. Never be alarmed by a sudden dash of color seemingly out of context. Say only to your questioning heart, "It is the Infinite wielding His brush; I know He does all things well."

*What good thing might God be creating
in my life right now?*

Prepare!

from *Make Haste My Beloved*

And God said unto Noah. . . .
Make thee an ark of gopher wood.
GENESIS 6:13–14

Your own future is shaped by today's decisions, therefore, the future should not be ignored as though irrelevant to today. Jesus did not teach man to ignore the future, but to prepare for it. His warning was against anxiety concerning tomorrow, not against preparation.

It was I who taught Noah to prepare for the flood. Draw on My wisdom, for to Me all things are plain now.

*What preparations should I be making
in my life now?*

There Is Always an Alternative

from *Progress of Another Pilgrim*

And he said, Take now thy son, thine only son
Isaac, whom thou lovest, and get thee into the
land of Moriah; and offer him there for a burnt
offering upon one of the mountains
which I will tell thee of.

GENESIS 22:2

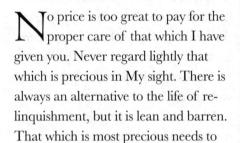

No price is too great to pay for the proper care of that which I have given you. Never regard lightly that which is precious in My sight. There is always an alternative to the life of re-linquishment, but it is lean and barren. That which is most precious needs to be offered up to Me continually.

My grace is as a beacon. It shall shed light on all that is now obscure.

What precious thing do I need
to offer up to God?

Relinquish Your Will

from *Come Away My Beloved*

And God sent me before you to preserve you a
posterity in the earth, and to save your lives by a
great deliverance.

GENESIS 45:7

My heart is grieved by your independence. How would Joseph have felt if his father and family had remained at home, starving in the famine, when he had invited them to share the bountiful stores he had at his disposal and desired to share freely with them?

Would he not have grieved far more deeply than over the unjust actions of his brothers who hated him? For to be rebuffed by a loved one causes pain not to be compared with the cruelties inflicted by an enemy.

*In what areas do I need to relinquish
my will to God?*

Release Others

from *Progress of Another Pilgrim*

But as for you, ye thought evil against me; but God
meant it unto good, to bring to pass, as it is this
day, to save much people alive.

GENESIS 50:20

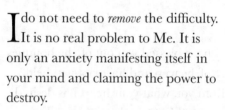

I do not need to *remove* the difficulty.
It is no real problem to Me. It is
only an anxiety manifesting itself in
your mind and claiming the power to
destroy.

I am restricted when you hold
negative thoughts about the actions
of other people. Release them to Me;
otherwise you turn the action upon
yourself to your own hurt.

*What negative thoughts might I be holding
toward other people's actions?*

January 6

Household Salvation

from Come Away My Beloved

For the LORD will pass through to smite the
Egyptians; and when he seeth the blood upon the
lintel, and on the two side posts, the LORD will
pass over the door, and will not suffer the destroyer
to come in unto your houses to smite you.

EXODUS 12:23

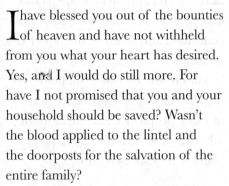

I have blessed you out of the bounties
of heaven and have not withheld
from you what your heart has desired.
Yes, and I would do still more. For
have I not promised that you and your
household should be saved? Wasn't
the blood applied to the lintel and
the doorposts for the salvation of the
entire family?

So renew your energies, and know
that I am working with you.

*What family member or friend might need my
prayers for salvation today?*

The Fear of God

from *Make Haste My Beloved*

Thou shalt have no other gods before me.

EXODUS 20:3

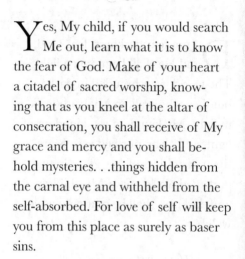

Yes, My child, if you would search Me out, learn what it is to know the fear of God. Make of your heart a citadel of sacred worship, knowing that as you kneel at the altar of consecration, you shall receive of My grace and mercy and you shall behold mysteries. . .things hidden from the carnal eye and withheld from the self-absorbed. For love of self will keep you from this place as surely as baser sins.

How can I make my heart a "citadel of sacred worship"?

The Kingdom of Lights

from Make Haste My Beloved

And he said, I beseech thee,
shew me thy glory.
EXODUS 33:18

———————— ∽ ————————

Do not fear darkness: fear God, and He shall be to you a light. The world is enshrouded in darkness, but they who walk in My truth walk in light. My kingdom is a kingdom of light, and clear, purified vessels are the transmitters of My glory in the darkened world. *Shine,* My children, and darkness shall be scattered as you walk!

*How can I shine God's light
into a dark world today?*

This Is the Glory Life

from *Dialogues with God*

For the cloud of the LORD was upon the taber-
nacle by day, and fire was on it by night, in the
sight of all the house of Israel,
throughout all their journeys.

EXODUS 40:38

Behold, I say unto thee, *This is the way, walk ye in it,* neither turn to the right hand nor to the left.

For I shall make the path for thy feet a plain path, and light shall be there, and there shall be the shining of My glory.

It shall not be the glory of man. It shall be the glory of God.

*How has God smoothed and lit
my path through life?*

January 10

The Oil of Consecration

from *Progress of Another Pilgrim*

In a pan it shall be made with oil; and when it is
baken, thou shalt bring it in: and the baken pieces
of the meat offering shalt thou offer for a sweet
savour unto the LORD. And the priest of his sons
that is anointed in his stead shall offer it: it is a
statute for ever unto the LORD; it shall be
wholly burnt.

LEVITICUS 6:21–22

A ll your ministry must be blessed
by the oil of consecration. Not
one thing can be withheld. That which
is most precious must be daily offered in dedication. Anything which is
unworthy or evil must be given to Me
so that it may be taken away; but the
pure and good must be given to Me
also, so that you may be continually
freed from clasping it to yourself.

Anything you grasp becomes a burden. Give all to Me in a daily morning
offering.

*What am I grasping that I should be
giving to God today?*

Obedience, the Fabric of Happiness

from Make Haste My Beloved

Ye shall do my judgments, and keep mine ordinances,
to walk therein: I am the LORD your God.

LEVITICUS 18:4

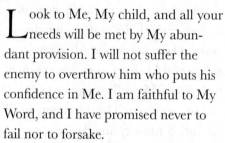

Look to Me, My child, and all your needs will be met by My abundant provision. I will not suffer the enemy to overthrow him who puts his confidence in Me. I am faithful to My Word, and I have promised never to fail nor to forsake.

Obedience is the fabric of happiness. To rebel is to seek sorrow. Only a yielded heart can find rest in Me; and to know contentment there must be resignation of personal rights in favor of My will.

*In what areas do I need to yield
my heart to God?*

Hold Your Ground

from On the Highroad of Surrender

Let us go up at once, and posess it, For we are well
able to overcome it.

NUMBERS 13:30

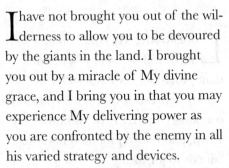

Ihave not brought you out of the wilderness to allow you to be devoured
by the giants in the land. I brought
you out by a miracle of My divine
grace, and I bring you in that you may
experience My delivering power as
you are confronted by the enemy in all
his varied strategy and devices.

Stretch forth the hand of faith. Set
foot upon the territory you wish to
claim. I will move ahead of you and
clear a path, but you must be determined to follow closely and to hold
your ground without wavering.

What territory do I wish to claim,
through faith in God?

Outer Blessing and Inner Strength

from *On the Highroad of Surrender*

But My servant Caleb, because he has a different
spirit in him and has followed Me fully,
I will bring into the land where he went,
and his descendants shall inherit it.

NUMBERS 14:24 NKJV

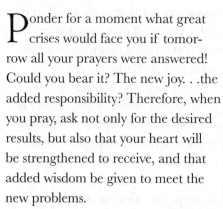

Ponder for a moment what great crises would face you if tomorrow all your prayers were answered! Could you bear it? The new joy. . .the added responsibility? Therefore, when you pray, ask not only for the desired results, but also that your heart will be strengthened to receive, and that added wisdom be given to meet the new problems.

You have watched some succeed only to fail. This occurs when outer blessings are sought and inner strength neglected.

What new challenges might my
answered prayers bring?

Whatsoever You Sow

from *Come Away My Beloved*

Be sure your sin will find you out.
NUMBERS 32:23

How can I give you healing for your body while there is anxiety in your mind? So long as there is disease in your thoughts, there will be disease in your body. One thing in particular you must develop for your own preservation, and that is an absolute confidence in My loving care.

Only when your mind is at rest can your body build health. Worry is an actively destructive force. Anxiety produces tension, and tension is the road to pain. Fear is devastating to the physical well-being of the body. Anger throws poison into the system that no antibiotic can ever counteract.

"Be sure your sin will find you out," the Bible states (Numbers 32:23). One of the most common ways that hidden sin is revealed is through the maladies of the body.

Where might my soul need healing?

My Holy Spirit Judges

from *Come Away My Beloved*

But if ye will not do so, behold, ye have sinned
against the LORD: and be sure your sin will
find you out.
NUMBERS 32:23

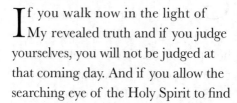

I f you walk now in the light of
My revealed truth and if you judge
yourselves, you will not be judged at
that coming day. And if you allow the
searching eye of the Holy Spirit to find
you out, then it will not be said to you,
"Your sin will find you out." Do not
resist Me or harden your hearts. Do
not provoke Me to use My chastening
rod, for I love you.

*In what ways have I resisted God's Holy
Spirit in "finding out" my sin?*

Give Me the Firstfruits

from Dialogues with God

Keep the sabbath day to sanctify it, as the LORD
thy God hath commanded thee.

DEUTERONOMY 5:12

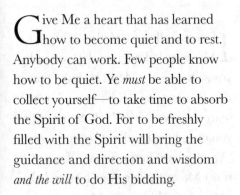

Give Me a heart that has learned
how to become quiet and to rest.
Anybody can work. Few people know
how to be quiet. Ye *must* be able to
collect yourself—to take time to absorb
the Spirit of God. For to be freshly
filled with the Spirit will bring the
guidance and direction and wisdom
and the will to do His bidding.

*In what ways should I quiet my heart
and rest?*

The Burden~Bearer

from *Come Away My Beloved*

He might prove thee, to do thee good
at thy latter end.
DEUTERONOMY 8:16

───────── ⟨✦⟩ ─────────

My child, do not share your burdens with all who come to you professing concern. I, Myself, am the great burden-bearer. You need not look to another. I will lead you and guide you in wisdom from above. All things will be as I plan them, if you allow Me the freedom to shape circumstances and lead you to the right decisions.

*What burdens should I hand over
to God today?*

Spiritual Liberty

from *On the Highroad of Surrender*

Arise, go over this Jordan, thou, and all this people,
unto the land which I do give to them, even to the
children of Israel.

Joshua 1:2

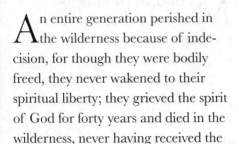

An entire generation perished in the wilderness because of indecision, for though they were bodily freed, they never wakened to their spiritual liberty; they grieved the spirit of God for forty years and died in the wilderness, never having received the promise (Hebrews 3:15–19).

Bringing you out, My children, is only the beginning. I am bringing sons to glory, and I am preparing a people who shall go in. They shall possess the land. They shall be strong in the Lord, and they shall fulfill My purposes (Joshua 1).

*What purposes might God
want to fulfill in me?*

A Spirit of Gratitude

from *Progress of Another Pilgrim*

Every place that the sole of your foot shall tread
upon, that have I given unto you,
as I said unto Moses.

JOSHUA 1:3

O My little one, the path has been prepared before you, and you shall not fear, neither hesitate. As you tread, you will find the victory has already been won. No challenge shall turn you aside, no past defeat shall dim your faith in My provision and grace.

Love Me with your whole heart. I am the Lord, your God. I have saved you and healed you, and you have much for which to praise Me. Never stop. The highest occupation of the soul is that of worship and adoration. Never cease to keep a spirit of over-flowing gratitude. It shall both sweeten your own spirit and lift your whole ministry into the highest plane.

Have I forgotten to thank God for anything?

January 20

He Has Filled My Cup

from Come Away My Beloved

And he said, Nay; but as captain of the host of the
LORD am I now come. And Joshua fell on his face
to the earth, and did worship, and said unto him,
What saith my Lord unto his servant?

JOSHUA 5:14

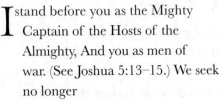

I stand before you as the Mighty
Captain of the Hosts of the
Almighty, And you as men of
war. (See Joshua 5:13–15.) We seek
no longer
To rest in green pastures and lie beside
still waters; For I have issued
my command to wipe out
the giants, And to utterly
destroy the inhabitants of the
land.

*What commands does the Mighty
Captain have for my life?*

Fear, a Sin

from *On the Highroad of Surrender*

Hebron therefore became the inheritance of Caleb
the son of Jephunneh the Kenezite unto this day,
because he wholly followed the LORD God of Israel.

JOSHUA 14:14

Be not faint of heart. Fear will rob
you of your possession as quickly
as any other sin; for truly fear is a sin
and it opens the door for many other
sins to follow.

Guard your heart from doubt and
every negative attitude. You cannot
afford to take the risk of entertaining
any such thoughts at so critical a time.
Only the strong in faith shall prevail.
Only those with a "Caleb" spirit shall
take the walled cities and crush out the
enemies.

Is mine a "Caleb" spirit?

Prepare!

from Make Haste My Beloved

And the LORD said unto Gideon, By the three
hundred men that lapped will I save you, and deliver
the Midianites into thine hand: and let all the other
people go every man unto his place.

JUDGES 7:7

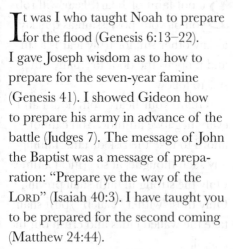

It was I who taught Noah to prepare
for the flood (Genesis 6:13–22).
I gave Joseph wisdom as to how to
prepare for the seven-year famine
(Genesis 41). I showed Gideon how
to prepare his army in advance of the
battle (Judges 7). The message of John
the Baptist was a message of preparation: "Prepare ye the way of the
LORD" (Isaiah 40:3). I have taught you
to be prepared for the second coming
(Matthew 24:44).

Yes, the riches of the future are for
those who make preparation today.
Draw on My wisdom, for to Me all
things are plain now.

*What wisdom do I need from God
to prepare for my future?*

You Shall Not Be Earthbound

from *Come Away My Beloved*

And Ruth said, . . .whither thou goest, I will go;
and where thou lodgest, I will lodge: thy people
shall be my people, and thy God my God.

RUTH 1:16

Receive My love freely. Drink of My Spirit. And mount up on the wings of My power. For there are powers of the air to be subdued and conquered. You need faith and the liberty and power of the Holy Spirit to overcome these and rise above them.

My Church shall be an overcoming church, and My Bride shall be a heavenly being. I will not choose a wife out of Egypt. I will take to Me one who has chosen to make My home her home and My people her people, even as Ruth did. But she who turns back, like Orpah, shall not enter into My inheritance.

Am I a Ruth or an Orpah?

Find Solitude

from Come Away My Beloved

O LORD of hosts, if thou wilt indeed look on the
affliction of thine handmaid, and remember me,
and not forget thine handmaid, but wilt give unto
thine handmaid a man child, then I will give him
unto the LORD all the days of his life, and there
shall no razor come upon his head.

1 SAMUEL 1:11

There is no blessing I would withhold from those who walk in
obedience to Me. Near to My heart
and precious in My sight are those
who have eyes to discern My purpose
and ears that listen to My direction.

Do not be intent on great accom-
plishments. By what standards do you
judge the importance of a matter?
It was a relatively small thing that
Hannah prayed for a son, but what
great things I accomplished through
Samuel!

*What small things can I offer up to
God today?*

Faith and the Delivering Angel

from *Progress of Another Pilgrim*

Thy servant slew both the lion and the bear: and this uncircumcised Philistine shall be as one of them, seeing he hath defied the armies of the living God.

1 SAMUEL 17:36

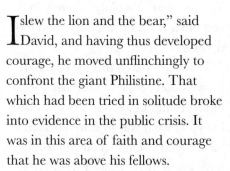

I slew the lion and the bear," said David, and having thus developed courage, he moved unflinchingly to confront the giant Philistine. That which had been tried in solitude broke into evidence in the public crisis. It was in this area of faith and courage that he was above his fellows.

Secret faith had its moment of open revelation. It is ever so. Build inner faith from the lesser challenges, and it will be your delivering angel in the most calamitous moment.

Am I building inner faith?

Recognize My Hand

from *Progress of Another Pilgrim*

He brought me forth also into a large place; he
delivered me, because he delighted in me.

2 SAMUEL 22:20

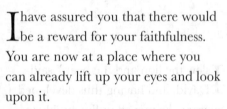

I have assured you that there would
be a reward for your faithfulness.
You are now at a place where you
can already lift up your eyes and look
upon it.

I have prepared this for you, and
I have stood beside you through the
times of endurance, and I have smiled,
knowing what was in store for you. I
have urged you on when you would
have given up, because I would not
allow you to fail.

Love Me more than ever. Recognize
My hand in this.

Have no fear. Your work is My
work, and I am well able to take care
of every aspect.

How has God's hand worked in my life?

A Living Sacrifice

from Come Away My Beloved

And the three mighty men. . .drew water out of
the well of Bethlehem. . .and brought it to David:
nevertheless he would not drink thereof, but
poured it out unto the LORD.

2 SAMUEL 23:16

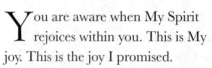

You are aware when My Spirit
rejoices within you. This is My
joy. This is the joy I promised.

This is the greatest joy that can
come to the human heart, for it is the
joy of God.

Surely you will not only rejoice but
be exceeding glad, with a gladness
surpassing your power to tell.

In this way you will give this back to
Me, even as David poured out to Me
the precious water from the well of
Bethlehem.

Am I pouring out my praise to the Lord?

January 28

Give Me a Drink

from Come Away My Beloved

And Elijah said unto her, Fear not; go and do as
thou hast said: but make me thereof a little cake
first, and bring it unto me, and after make for thee
and for thy son.

1 KINGS 17:13

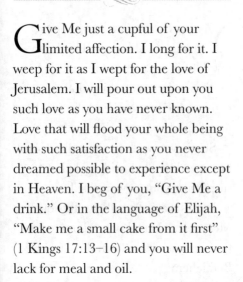

Give Me just a cupful of your limited affection. I long for it. I weep for it as I wept for the love of Jerusalem. I will pour out upon you such love as you have never known. Love that will flood your whole being with such satisfaction as you never dreamed possible to experience except in Heaven. I beg of you, "Give Me a drink." Or in the language of Elijah, "Make me a small cake from it first" (1 Kings 17:13–16) and you will never lack for meal and oil.

Does God have my affection?

Be Responsive

from *Progress of Another Pilgrim*

And he said, Go forth, and stand upon the mount
before the LORD. And, behold, the LORD passed
by, and a great and strong wind rent the mountains,
and brake in pieces the rocks before the LORD;
but the LORD was not in the wind.

1 KINGS 19:11

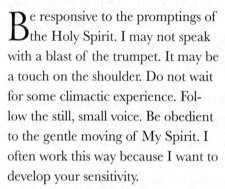

B e responsive to the promptings of
the Holy Spirit. I may not speak
with a blast of the trumpet. It may be
a touch on the shoulder. Do not wait
for some climactic experience. Follow the still, small voice. Be obedient
to the gentle moving of My Spirit. I
often work this way because I want to
develop your sensitivity.

I know your frailties, but in this
way I purpose to make you strong. By
working with you in this quiet fashion,
I would strengthen your faith.

Am I responding to His still, small voice?

Protection

from On the Highroad of Surrender

And the LORD opened the eyes of the young man;
and he saw: and, behold, the mountain was full of
horses and chariots of fire round about Elisha.

2 KINGS 6:17

─────── ∼ ───────

My protection is all you need,
My child. The help of others is
vain. But all will fall into place beauti-
fully as you rest it in My hands. Fear
not that any can harm you.

Gehazi owed his own safety to
Elisha, for God was with Elisha in the
form of an angelic host that filled the
mountains, and Gehazi, the servant,
benefited by being in his company. So
shall it be for those who journey with
you, as God, seeing your confidence in
Him and desire to please Him and do
His will, moves in your behalf.

Cast fear forever from your heart.

*When have I experienced God's
protection?*

January 31

End-Time Tensions

from *On the Highroad of Surrender*

And it shall be, when you hear a sound of marching
in the tops of the mulberry trees, then you shall go
out to battle, for God has gone out before you to
strike the camp of the Philistines.

1 CHRONICLES 14:15 NKJV

My grace and mercy are intensi-
fied, not in spite of, but because
of the tensions of the end-time. My
love is moving in surrendered hearts
and producing a quality of dedication,
zeal, and awareness unsurpassed in
the spiritual heroes of the past.

Lift up your heads: Lift up your
hearts. Let your faith and courage be
reinforced. For in the Spirit you shall
listen and hear the sound of a great
army readying for battle, and there
shall be the sound of going in the tops
of the mulberry trees, and they who
have been enlisted by the Spirit shall
go forth conquering and to conqueror.

What role will I play in God's battle?

Motivation

from *Progress of Another Pilgrim*

If my people, which are called by my name,
shall humble themselves, and pray, and seek my face,
and turn from their wicked ways; then will I hear
from heaven, and will forgive their sin,
and will heal their land.

2 CHRONICLES 7:14

Confession, repentance, and prayer strengthen the will to move in the direction of holiness. No one is brought into a life of holiness by outside force. The inner desire is always the first and the foremost motivation. As soon as the desire for righteousness is present, the Holy Spirit will immediately fill it with His own energy and bring the soul into victory.

What do I need to confess, repent of, and pray over?

Deliverance Has Come

from *Make Haste My Beloved*

And when they began to sing and to praise, the
LORD set ambushments against [their enemies].
2 CHRONICLES 20:22

Yes, and I have set ambushments against your enemies, and I will smite him that causes you to dwell in fear. I will not suffer your foot to be moved but will cause you to walk in the way I have designed for you and no man shall hinder. For I have set My battle in array, and I, the Lord your God, will fight for you and you shall hold your peace.

You shall rejoice and sing, yes, you can dance for joy, for your deliverance has already come, and the day of your visitation is here!

In what ways has God delivered me?

Devotion and Warfare

from *On the Highroad of Surrender*

Every one of the builders had his sword girded at
his side as he built. And the one who sounded the
trumpet was beside me.

NEHEMIAH 4:18 NKJV

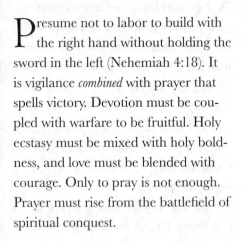

Presume not to labor to build with
the right hand without holding the
sword in the left (Nehemiah 4:18). It
is vigilance *combined* with prayer that
spells victory. Devotion must be cou-
pled with warfare to be fruitful. Holy
ecstasy must be mixed with holy bold-
ness, and love must be blended with
courage. Only to pray is not enough.
Prayer must rise from the battlefield of
spiritual conquest.

*How well do I handle God's "sword"—
His Word?*

Find Solitude

from *Come Away My Beloved*

Forty years You sustained them in the
wilderness; They lacked nothing.

NEHEMIAH 9:21 NKJV

My Truth abides forever, and no
one will escape, for it will be
as a flaming sword as it proceeds out
of My mouth. For in judgment I will
come, to purge the world and to set up
My Kingdom.

Do not resist Me or harden your
hearts. I take no pleasure in the affliction of My children. In love I chasten
to prevent the deeper suffering in-
volved should I allow you to go on in
a path of evil. But My heart is glad
when you walk close, with your hand
in Mine, and we may talk over the
plans for each day's journey and activities so that it becomes a happy way
that we travel in mutual fellowship.

So pour out your praise to Me from
a light heart. I will plan your path, and
we will go singing.

Is my heart hard or tender?

February 5

A Secret Process

from *On the Highroad of Surrender*

Every maid's turn was come to go in to king
Ahasuerus, after that she had been twelve months,
according to the manner of the women, (for so
were the days of their purifications accomplished.)

ESTHER 2:12

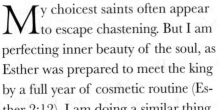

My choicest saints often appear
to escape chastening. But I am
perfecting inner beauty of the soul, as
Esther was prepared to meet the king
by a full year of cosmetic routine (Esther 2:12). I am doing a similar thing
with My Church. My Bride is undergoing her beautification in anticipation
of the coming of the Bridegroom.

This is why she must be drawn
aside. This is a ministry to her inner
soul, and I have ordained special ones
to carry out this work of preparing
the Bride. I commend you into their
hands and their ministrations. Only so
can you be presented before the King,
purged of flaws and imperfections.

How has God beautified my soul?

I Have Built a Hedge

from *Progress of Another Pilgrim*

Hast not thou made an hedge about him, and
about his house, and about all that he hath
on every side?

JOB 1:10

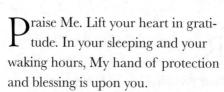

P raise Me. Lift your heart in gratitude. In your sleeping and your
waking hours, My hand of protection
and blessing is upon you.

I have built a hedge about you, even
as was written concerning Job. This
was not a false accusation of the devil
to Job: It was an actual reality. I only
removed it to test and to prove him
and to put to silence the enemy of his
soul. But for multitudes of My children,
I have never removed the hedge. I am
keeping you, My child, and for one
purpose in particular—that you be
able to accomplish the task committed
to you. Therefore, give diligence to
your mission.

When has God placed a hedge
around me?

February 7

An Uncomplaining Heart

from On the Highroad of Surrender

Behold, happy is the man whom God corrects;
Therefore do not despise the chastening of the
Almighty. For He bruises, but He binds up; He
wounds, but His hands make whole.

JOB 5:17–18 NKJV

Be patient while I deal with you in the areas of your own inner needs. Bear joyfully My rod of correction. Know that while I minister to you, you are being prepared to minister to others. Make no mistake, there cannot be one without the other. Your attitudes need the disciplining of the Holy Spirit.

Rest in Me in the quiet place and give Me an uncomplaining heart. I will fill it with My Grace. When I see that you are ready to do it, I will make My will inescapable.

Are there complaints in my heart?

Affliction, No Stranger

from *On the Highroad of Surrender*

Though He slay me, yet will I trust Him.
Even so, I will defend my own ways before Him.

JOB 13:15 NKJV

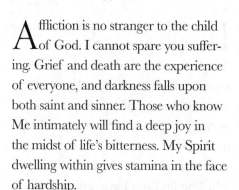

Affliction is no stranger to the child
of God. I cannot spare you suffering. Grief and death are the experience
of everyone, and darkness falls upon
both saint and sinner. Those who know
Me intimately will find a deep joy in
the midst of life's bitterness. My Spirit
dwelling within gives stamina in the face
of hardship.

I do not smooth out the way for My
loved ones, for how then could they
testify of My provision? Better your lips
were sealed forever than that they should
deny Me in the hour of calamity.

I prepare you in order to use you
in the hour of crisis. The crisis is
not the time to cry for deliverance,
saying, "Lord, save me," but to cry,
"Lord, use me."

How does want to God use me?

Inner Calm

from *On the Highroad of Surrender*

"Now acquaint yourself with Him, and be at
peace; Thereby good will come to you."
JOB 22:21 NKJV

Let nothing disturb your quietness
of spirit, for from the place of
inner calm you draw courage to move
forward through all obstacles. I am
never the source of turbulence. You
may react with turbulence when I am
dealing with your soul, but whenever
you do so, it is because your will is in
rebellion and you have stiffened your
neck. My disciplines are received with
peace in the heart that is submissive to
My will.

Never console the one who pines
under My chastening rod lest you
hinder the work of grace I am doing
in his heart and become an obstacle to
his spiritual growth.

How well do I accept God's discipline?

The Simplicity of Obedience

from Progress of Another Pilgrim

And unto man he said, Behold, the fear of the
LORD, that is wisdom; and to depart from
evil is understanding.

JOB 28:28 NKJV

You need not search for answers to the many mysteries of life, but only trust and follow Me in the simplicity of obedience. Understanding will come to you as you walk in obedience.

Make Me your goal, and wisdom shall be given each day as needed. Do not try to reverse the order.

What is my true goal in life?

Unseen Companionship

from *On the Highroad of Surrender*

Preserve me, O God, for in You

I put my trust.

PSALM 16:1 NKJV

Courage, My child! No hand shall sustain you but Mine own. Hoped you for another? Disappointment awaits every soul not sustained by My love. Never draw from other sources, for when you do, you rob the life force from another, leaving him weaker and yourself deceived; for you confuse comfort with strength.

Fellowship is not life. It is to be given rather than sought. It is shared in the overflow. The soul that has been enriched by communion with God will not be dismayed by isolation, but will welcome solitude. He will seek not the crowd but the closet, and emerging will never walk alone, for he has always unseen companionship, and whoever joins him on the way will be doubly blessed.

How have I been enriched by communion with God?

The Comfort of My Presence

from *On the Highroad of Surrender*

For You will light my lamp;
The LORD my God will enlighten my darkness.
For by You I can run against a troop,
By my God I can leap over a wall.

PSALM 18:28–29 NKJV

Over and over have I reassured you of My love for you. More than all the comforts of the world, I want you to know the comfort of My presence.

Many dangers beset your path, but I shall keep you if you trust in Me. Many sorrows compass you about, but I give you joy that is greater. Darkness presses you, and doubts arise, but My light, the light of My Holy Spirit, ever burns within your heart to cheer you and encourage you to go on, yes, to go on knowing surely I will bring you out.

Do I have God's greater joy?

A Holy Temple

from *On the Highroad of Surrender*

Who may ascend into the hill of the LORD?
Or who may stand in His holy place?
He who has clean hands and a pure heart.
PSALM 24:3–4 NKJV

Your heart, My child, is the citadel of the Holy Spirit. No evil shall dwell there as long as you allow Me to rule and reign. I hold the keys to every chamber and will keep out every evil thing if you do not invite the enemy. I desire for you a holy temple.

Let not your worship be tinged with carnality. Give Me your adoration from a pure heart and let no ulterior motives invade your personal sanctuary, for I desire truth in the depths of the soul and the divided heart cannot worship.

How pure is my heart?

The Quiet Spirit

from *On the Highroad of Surrender*

Who may ascend into the hill of the LORD?
Or who may stand in His holy place?
He who has clean hands and a pure heart,
Who has not lifted up his soul to an idol,
Nor sworn deceitfully.
He shall receive blessing from the LORD,
And righteousness from the God of his
salvation.

PSALM 24:3–5 NKJV

B e silent when you come to Me. Only the quiet spirit enters the place of communion. Strivings are left outside. Vexations bar the door, for they are caused by reactions to things, places, and people, and none of these are related to worship. They are related to the flesh. Put them out of the temple. They that have clean hands and a pure heart shall ascend unto the mountain of the Lord. When you are loosed from the earthly, then shall the heavenly be revealed.

What bars the door to my worship?

The Father's House

from *On the Highroad of Surrender*

One thing I have desired of the LORD,
That will I seek:
That I may dwell in the house of the LORD
All the days of my life,
To behold the beauty of the LORD,
And to inquire in His temple.

PSALM 27:4 NKJV

In My Father's house are many mansions, and there is a place for you, My child. Look not for a place in the world. Your place is in the Father's house. Your soul can rest even now only in the place I provide.

Your restlessness is due to your involvement in things other than My ordained will for you. You are not of the world, even as I was not of the world. The spirit is nourished only by the eternal, and in prayer the soul breathes the atmosphere of heaven.

How much am I resting in the Father's will?

Angels Assist You

from On the Highroad of Surrender

I will extol You, O LORD, for You have lifted me
up, And have not let my foes rejoice over me. . . .
I cried out to You, And You healed me.

PSALM 30:1–2 NKJV

O My child, do not weep. I am doing a beautiful work. Stress and
pressure and pain are often the path to
victory and understanding.

I am in the midst, and I am a strong
deliverer. You need not be concerned.
Courage is the greatest contribution you can make at this point. To
be strong now will make the path of
recovery easier. Faith is an essential
ingredient in every solution. . .often it
is the solution itself.

Never underestimate the power of
faith. Hold fast. Trust. Unseen angels
assist you. Doors are opening to let
you pass into safety.

Am I trusting God now?

Rejoice Always

from *On the Highroad of Surrender*

I will bless the LORD at all times;
His praise shall continually be in my mouth.
PSALM 34:1 NKJV

Knowing that I love you at all times will bring comfort in the hours when you need it most. Be obedient to My command that you rejoice in the Lord always. Because I must become your one true source of life and joy, I allow the difficult circumstances to come. Through them, I test your love for Me. It is not a time for you to test My love for you! My love for you is constant and is not to be reckoned by your own happiness or unhappiness. I send all in love. If you have unhappiness, it is because of your own wrong reactions.

Learn to react rightly and to properly discern My intention. Never blame Me for your misery, for it is not from My hand.

How can I discern God's intention?

Contentment

from *On the Highroad of Surrender*

Many are the afflictions of the righteous,
But the LORD delivers him out of them all.
PSALM 34:19 NKJV

My children do not enjoy immunity to trouble, but in the midst of each painful experience My Spirit is at work fashioning beauty in the soul.

Be patient in tribulation and I will minister My grace to you and your heart will rejoice, yes, more than in the day of pleasantness. For when outer blessings are withheld, inner peace is deepened, for the soul turns to worship with less distraction.

Disappointment is foreign to the Spirit, for it has no part in faith. The trusting soul possesses all things in Christ and looks not to others for blessing: therefore he can never be disappointed. Joy and contentment crown his head, and peace reigns in his heart.

Am I joyful and contented, or disappointed?

Loose the Child

from *On the Highroad of Surrender*

Cast your burden on the LORD,
And He shall sustain you;
He shall never permit the righteous to be moved.

PSALM 55:22 NKJV

The little ones are in My care; you shall not be anxious. He carries the lambs in His bosom. Surely, it is true. Rely on Me for I am ever watchful, and the tenderness of My love exceeds that of a mother.

Picture the Lord Jesus as He took the young children upon His knee and blessed them. I say to you, He is the same today, and His compassion fathomless. Trustingly place your child in His hands. They are healing hands, and you may count on Him to bring wholeness and perfection, whether here or in the Father's house.

Your heart is bound to the heart of the child. Loose the cord of affection lest it break.

Can I trust God with my child?

Trust

from *On the Highroad of Surrender*

In God I have put my trust;
I will not be afraid.
What can man do to me?
PSALM 56:11 NKJV

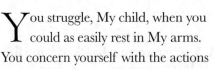

You struggle, My child, when you could as easily rest in My arms. You concern yourself with the actions of others and neglect the only important thing: to abide in Me. He who abides in me has no need to be anxious.

When you are moving out of My divine will, you have unrest. Abiding brings confiding, for to know Me is to trust Me, and trust brings peace. Your trust in Me is colored by human experience. This should never be allowed to happen. Though all men fail, I am no less faithful: indeed, in the face of human disappointments your trust in Me becomes even more vital.

To understand is to believe, and to believe is to trust.

How vital is my trust in Him?

Living in Joy

from On the Highroad of Surrender

Let them be confounded and consumed who are
adversaries of my life; Let them be covered with
reproach and dishonor who seek my hurt. But
I will hope continually, and will praise You yet
more and more.

PSALM 71:13–14 NKJV

When you are baptized into His
Spirit, evil loses its power to
destroy you, darkness is dispelled, and
the broken spirit healed. Joy is a balm
that soothes the soul and lifts the burden from the grieving heart. Joy will
be your saving grace, and praise your
meat and drink. Only a joyful heart
can worship Me in a way pleasing in
My sight.

To weep and mourn is needless
waste.

Am I mourning or rejoicing today?

Maintain Constancy

from On the Highroad of Surrender

For He satisfies the longing soul,
And fills the hungry soul with goodness.
PSALM 107:9 NKJV

Do not grieve, My child, though all you hold dear be taken from you. You have need of nothing. Hold Me close to your heart, and I will satisfy every longing. Allow Me to comfort you, and you will find yourself reaching out less and less to others for support and solace.

My presence will sustain you, but only if you maintain a closeness of relationship. Pure neglect alone can cause you to lose this as much as open sin.

Maintain a constancy in devotion, and I will be pleased and will do all manner of wonderful things in your behalf. I will cause blessings to be heaped upon you. You will be increased abundantly in the riches of the Kingdom.

How constant is my devotion?

The Romance of the Spirit

from On the Highroad of Surrender

Blessed are the undefiled in the way,
Who walk in the law of the LORD!
Blessed are those who keep His testimonies,
Who seek Him with the whole heart.

PSALM 119:1–2 NKJV

There is a path of service in which I would lead you. No foot has preceded you there. It is virgin territory. It is My own special way for you. It is a way of romance—the Romance of the Spirit.

My love for you is deeper than you have comprehended. As you walk on into fuller commitment, and as you are less hampered by the things of the world, I will give you deeper insight and more complete revelations of Myself.

When you have given up everything, we will be able to go forth together, and you will experience an inner power that you were not able to find before.

How completely do I seek to serve God?

Harmony with the Message

from On the Highroad of Surrender

I will run the course of Your commandments,
For You shall enlarge my heart.
PSALM 119:32 NKJV

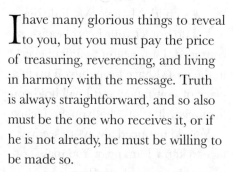

I have many glorious things to reveal to you, but you must pay the price of treasuring, reverencing, and living in harmony with the message. Truth is always straightforward, and so also must be the one who receives it, or if he is not already, he must be willing to be made so.

You cannot perfect your own righteousness. I must do it for you, but I need your consent. I need your desire to be made holy. Surely I will answer when you call, and I will work in patience and in gentleness, but I will not stop until the perfecting process is finished.

Do I desire to be holy?

Constancy

from On the Highroad of Surrender

Indeed, the darkness shall not hide from You,
But the night shines as the day;
The darkness and the light are both alike to You.
PSALM 139:12 NKJV

———————— ∽ ————————

My child, My love, My little one, do not let your heart be discouraged. I am nearer you than ever in the past. I have brought you up to a place of constancy, and I will hold you firm regardless of what you are feeling.

You do not need always to see My face to know I am near. You may touch My face to know I am near. You may touch My hand by faith in moments when it is too dark to see anything. Never let darkness frighten you. My Spirit is everywhere. . .even in the darkness.

When I fear, do I reach out to God or something else?

Trim Your Wick

from *On the Highroad of Surrender*

Search me, O God, and know my heart. . .see if
there is any wicked way in me, and lead me in the
way everlasting.

PSALM 139:23–24 NKJV

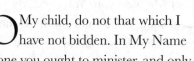

O My child, do not that which I
have not bidden. In My Name
alone you ought to minister, and only
when your own soul is free can the
Spirit move unhindered.

Not only is time wasted when
you disobey Me, but many souls are
damaged, and your own no less.

Never try to evaluate a situation.
Obey Me. It is difficult only to be obedient. How can you presume to handle
any more?

Trim your wick and polish your
lamp. Your light is growing dim. Come
back to listening only to My voice.

I love you and I have chosen and
trained you to do the tasks I have ordained. Be content with nothing less.

How obedient have I been to God?

February 27

Unquestioning Trust

from Progress of Another Pilgrim

Trust in the LORD with all thine heart; and lean
not unto thine own understanding.

PROVERBS 3:5

L et Me bless you. You need My
blessing more than you need the
help of all others combined. How
often have I asked you to follow Me? I
look to see you following, and instead I
see you standing still and reckoning—
or worse, fainting by the wayside.

It is your total commitment for
which I wait. It is your unquestioning
trust for which I yearn. It is your love
flowing in utter simplicity which alone
opens your channel to receive My
mercies.

You can turn your burdens into
blessings by giving Me everything.

Am I totally committed to God?

The Language of Love

from *On the Highroad of Surrender*

Keep your heart with all diligence,
For out of it spring the issues of life.
PROVERBS 4:23 NKJV

Be silent, My child, and when you speak, let it be your heart that calls My name. Many have My name upon their lips but their hearts are a hollow shell. Love is not in a mouth that is full, but in an overflowing heart.

With the heart man believes unto righteousness, and with the mouth he confesses unto salvation (Romans 10:10). No mouth shall testify of salvation and speak the truth until first the heart has believed unto righteousness.

I listen for the words of your heart. I understand the language of love.

When you listen for My voice, listen with your heart.

*What do I need to "tune out" to
hear God with my heart?*

Do Not Gather Fire

from On the Highroad of Surrender

Can a man take fire to his bosom,
and his clothes not be burned?

PROVERBS 6:27 NKJV

H ave I not said you should pray
much that you might not enter
into temptation? You are in My care at
all times, but some stresses put upon the
soul could be avoided by not presuming
upon My grace.

I desire always to help, but many
pray too late; for by their own careless
actions they have placed their feet in a
slippery path, and the results are almost
inevitable. Prayer at this point is like
seeking guidance when the route has
been predetermined by self-will and the
destination is already in sight.

Do not gather fire into your garments
and pray not to be burned, nor take up
a serpent and ask for protection. Give
the devil wide berth, and spare the soul
much unnecessary anguish.

How wide a berth have I given the devil?

Learn to Listen

from On the Highroad of Surrender

In the multitude of words sin is not lacking,
but he who restrains his lips is wise.

PROVERBS 10:19 NKJV

When you pray, My child, do not make it a one-way conversation. Know I am listening, but know also I will respond and will speak to you if you give Me opportunity. Prayer is not only of the lips, but of the ear also, for prayer is of the heart, and the heart that has learned to love has learned to listen more than to speak!

A loving heart will teach you this. Speaking is often motivated by self-seeking, self-preservation, self-defense, self-aggrandizement and every other expression of the ego. Listening is an expression of interest and concern for others.

When you come to Me in prayer, you ought to come to enjoy Me, not to entertain Me. A lack of humility causes you to be verbally expansive.

Am I listening in prayer?

True Peace and False

from *Progress of Another Pilgrim*

There is a way which seemeth right unto a man,
but the end thereof are the ways of death.

PROVERBS 14:12

Peace is in the full expression of
My will. Anything short of this is
a false peace. There is a dullness of
spirit. . .a sort of stupor that overtakes
the one who is no longer spiritually
sensitive. This is often mistaken for
true peace in a way that can be compared to the freezing man who feels
sleepy, not knowing he is slipping into
the very jaws of death.

Let not this sort of thing befall you.
Make sure that your peace is the result
of actively being in the will of God,
and permit yourself no indulgence in
selfishness.

How much of God's peace am I experiencing?

Godly Sorrow Versus Carnal

from *Progress of Another Pilgrim*

A merry heart maketh a cheerful countenance:
but by sorrow of the heart the spirit is broken.
PROVERBS 15:13

O vermuch sorrow causes the heart to fail. If you would be a rejoicing Christian, the griefs of the carnal man must be laid aside. There are sufferings of spirit through which every soul must pass in the process of perfection, but these are not to be compared to the complaints laid upon the soul which are directly related to uncrucified affections.

To bemoan any unpleasant natural circumstance accomplishes nothing but a heaping up of misery. Undue distress about untoward happenings is devastating to the soul. The only kind of sorrow that I can use for your good is the godly sorrow of true repentance.

Turn to Me in every trial, and give it all to Me.

What trials are in my life today?

Frugality and Supply

from Progress of Another Pilgrim

Better is little with the fear of the LORD than great
treasure and trouble therewith.

PROVERBS 15:16

———————— ∼ ————————

You shall have My blessing as you
bear the yoke, and in carrying
My burdens there shall always be joy. I
have called you for this ministry, and I
will supply your needs so that you will
not be weighed down with financial
cares. Be willing to do without until I
supply. Such as is needful I will give,
and anything more would be a snare
and a disappointment.

Luxuries burden the soul with
guilt. Learn to discern the difference
between necessities and luxuries, and
be content with modest things.

Leave off indulgences and follow the pattern of others who have
learned this lesson. Let your soul be
inspired by the character of those who
are disciplined in frugality.

How can I be disciplined in frugality?

A Merry Heart

from *On the Highroad of Surrender*

A merry heart does good, like medicine.
PROVERBS 17:22 NKJV

To mourn adversity multiplies the misfortune. It is not hypocrisy to rejoice in distress: It is obedience; for, says the Scripture, "Rejoice in the Lord always and again, I say, Rejoice" (Philippians 4:4).

Nothing is gained, but much is lost by bitterness of spirit in the day of trouble. You may not be able to escape calamity, but you should even more avoid a doleful countenance because it denotes a tempest in the heart and turbulence of mind, and reveals rebellion against the hand of God as it shapes destiny.

Look unto Jesus, "the author and finisher of our faith" (Hebrews 12:2). In Him dwells only that which is of the light. Peace, joy, and hope are His mantle, and holiness emanates from His presence.

Have I learned to rejoice in distress?

March 6

Wisdom, a Gift

from On the Highroad of Surrender

He who goes about as a talebearer reveals secrets;
Therefore do not associate with one who
flatters with his lips.
PROVERBS 20:19 NKJV

———————— ❧ ————————

Much false doctrine has been
generated out of man's fleshly
desire to possess knowledge not yet
revealed. In his impertinence, he has
resented even the silence of God
and expressed his intolerance of this
silence by fabricating ideas of his own
to fill the vacuum of ignorance.

O foolish creature! To have the
mind filled with information is a
questionable blessing. Knowledge and
wisdom are gifts from God. Information wrongly acquired or inaccurately
interpreted becomes a curse rather
than a blessing. Be content to know
only what is freely revealed by either
God or man, and be not a scavenger
of worthless information.

*How am I using God's gifts of
knowledge and wisdom?*

Indolence

from *Progress of Another Pilgrim*

I went by the field of the slothful. . .it was all
grown over with thorns, and nettles had covered
the face thereof, and the stone wall thereof was
broken down.

PROVERBS 24:30–31

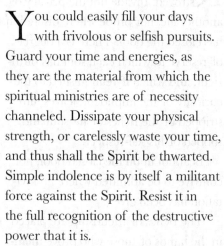

You could easily fill your days
with frivolous or selfish pursuits.
Guard your time and energies, as
they are the material from which the
spiritual ministries are of necessity
channeled. Dissipate your physical
strength, or carelessly waste your time,
and thus shall the Spirit be thwarted.
Simple indolence is by itself a militant
force against the Spirit. Resist it in
the full recognition of the destructive
power that it is.

Determine in your heart to respond immediately to every prompting of the Spirit. Never dispute, for
He is always right, and there can be
no ramifications.

What kind of pursuits fill my days?

Withdraw Your Foot

from *On the Highroad of Surrender*

Where there is no wood, the fire goes out;
and where there is no talebearer, strife ceases.

PROVERBS 26:20 NKJV

Robbed of privacy, friendship is destroyed. Invade not the privacy of another life, nor probe where discretion has closed the door. There is a degree of reserve to which each soul has birthright, and which if relinquished to the curiosity of the impudent, leaves him stripped of the riches of his soul and robbed of his self-respect.

Beat not upon the closed door, nor contrive to be admitted where no invitation has been given.

The riches of friendship are placed in the hands of those who prove themselves trustworthy. The ignorant will rob a nest of its eggs. The wise wait patiently for the sound of baby birds. He who steals the eggs deprives himself of this pleasure.

What kind of friend am I?

Inner Strength and Outer Action

from *Progress of Another Pilgrim*

He that covereth his sins shall not prosper:
but whoso confesseth and forsaketh them
shall have mercy.

PROVERBS 28:13

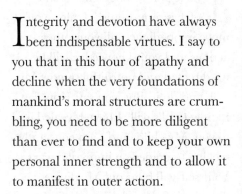

Integrity and devotion have always been indispensable virtues. I say to you that in this hour of apathy and decline when the very foundations of mankind's moral structures are crumbling, you need to be more diligent than ever to find and to keep your own personal inner strength and to allow it to manifest in outer action.

How much integrity and devotion
characterize my life?

March 10

A Yielded Spirit

from *On the Highroad of Surrender*

He who is often rebuked, and hardens his neck,
will suddenly be destroyed,
and that without remedy.

PROVERBS 29:1 NKJV

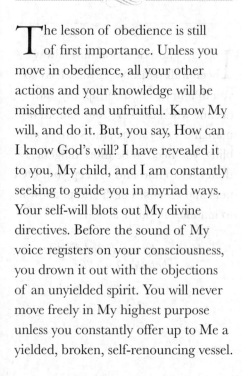

The lesson of obedience is still of first importance. Unless you move in obedience, all your other actions and your knowledge will be misdirected and unfruitful. Know My will, and do it. But, you say, How can I know God's will? I have revealed it to you, My child, and I am constantly seeking to guide you in myriad ways. Your self-will blots out My divine directives. Before the sound of My voice registers on your consciousness, you drown it out with the objections of an unyielded spirit. You will never move freely in My highest purpose unless you constantly offer up to Me a yielded, broken, self-renouncing vessel.

Am I a yielded vessel?

Bread Upon the Waters

from *Come Away My Beloved*

Cast your bread upon the waters,
for you will find it after many days.
ECCLESIASTES 11:1 NKJV

Do not be afraid to follow Me, nor draw back in doubt. I will provide all that you lack, and I will pave the way for you with My bounty.

You are not treading alone. There are many with you on the same road. It is the road of faith and trust, and you will have sweet fellowship, for there are others who will join you in this walk.

You will rejoice with exceeding joy, and your joy shall be shared by angels. They walk beside you and guard your way.

Never limit Me. I will take you through, though cliffs should rise before you. There will always be a provision, and in My mercy I will see that you find it.

How has God provided for me during my Christian walk?

Praise and Reproof

from *Come Away My Beloved*

Behold, you are fair, my love!
Behold, you are fair!
<small>SONG OF SOLOMON 1:15 NKJV</small>

My child, do not let the words of others influence you unduly—neither their praise nor their criticism. Weigh each for its proper value, and come back to Me. Only in communion with Me can you be sure of the truth. If I correct you, it is for your betterment. If I encourage you, it is because I know you need it.

If you accept My love and approval, you will be given courage to face your sins and faults. The more you find of the truth about your own self, the more you will be set free from improper evaluations of your worth, free from false pride that seeks to cover recognized flaws.

I want your life, character, and personality to be as beautiful and lovely as I visualized you to be when I created you.

*Have I truly accepted God's love
and approval?*

God's Heart

from Come Away My Beloved

My beloved spake, and said unto me,
Rise up, my love, my fair one, and come away.
SONG OF SOLOMON 2:10

I love you, and if you can always, as it were, feel My pulse beat, you will receive insight that will give you sustaining strength. I bore your sins and I wish to carry your burdens. You may take the gift of a light and merry heart, for My love dispels all fear and is a cure for every ill. Lay your head upon My breast and lose yourself in Me. You will experience resurrection life and peace; the joy of the Lord will become your strength; and wells of salvation will be opened within you (see Song of Solomon 2:9–13).

Are the wells of salvation opened in me?

Immediate Obedience

from *On the Highroad of Surrender*

If you are willing and obedient,
you shall eat the good of the land.

ISAIAH 1:19 NKJV

—————— ❧ ——————

You never enhance either your own life nor the lives of others if you are out of My perfect will. When I give you guidance and you are persuaded in your own mind of My leading, never ponder your decision. There is but one possible reply, and that is "Yes, Lord." Then simply do My bidding, and do it immediately.

Much confusion and remorse would be averted if all My children acted in this manner. This is why delayed obedience is nearly always disobedience, because along with the procrastination there is deliberation followed by rationalization, and by the time decision finally evolves into action, your own will is in control.

How often do I delay my obedience?

The Seeds of the Word

from *Progress of Another Pilgrim*

I heard the voice of the Lord, saying, Whom shall
I send, and who will go for us? Then said I,
Here am I; send me.

ISAIAH 6:8

Lo, the message is Mine, but I
have need of those who will
speak it without alteration and without any attempt to please men.

I have much to say that is not
pleasant to hear, because the heart of
man has grown fat with self-interest,
and the light of the knowledge of the
things of God has grown dim.

The seeds of the Word have long
since dried up and died in many a
prayerless life. I need those who will
speak it again and send it out afresh
in the dynamic power of the Holy
Spirit. The Word must be spoken
through those who are spiritually
alive, otherwise it loses its power to
produce new life.

Am I willing to accurately speak God's truth?

Learn Well and Listen Closely

from *Progress of Another Pilgrim*

Thou wilt keep him in perfect peace, whose mind
is stayed on thee: because he trusteth in thee.

ISAIAH 26:3

No disturbance, either in yourself or in others, can interfere with the moving of My Spirit if you do not focus attention upon it.

Be as a babe in its mother's arms and know that I carry you near to My heart, and this is why you have knowledge of many things not revealed to others. They must find this place for themselves before they can hear My voice. Meanwhile, you are My ambassador to them.

Learn well, and listen closely.

*What kind of an ambassador
have I been for God?*

An Instrument of Praise

from Come Away My Beloved

In returning and rest you shall be saved;
In quietness and confidence shall be your strength.

ISAIAH 30:15 NKJV

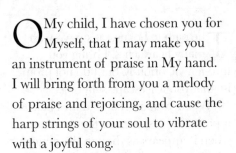

O My child, I have chosen you for Myself, that I may make you an instrument of praise in My hand. I will bring forth from you a melody of praise and rejoicing, and cause the harp strings of your soul to vibrate with a joyful song.

Bless Me with your lips, and whisper My Name in adoration. I will free you from the prison house, and you will exalt your God in liberty of spirit.

Do not turn back in unbelief, but press onward and upward until the darkness is left behind and you come out into the light. You will see Me then face-to-face, and know Me as your dearest friend.

What kind of praise instrument am I?

Release Your Tensions

from *On the Highroad of Surrender*

The work of righteousness will be peace,
and the effect of righteousness, quietness and
assurance forever.

Isaiah 32:17 nkjv

———————

The path to holiness is strewn with many heartaches. I bring you through victoriously, but I do not promise that you will escape suffering.

When you are rebuffed and bear it patiently, yes, even in the moment when it appears as though the actions of others prevent the fulfillment of your own inner vision, be assured, My child, of My understanding and patience, and know that I am a harmonizing influence.

Even your zeal to please Me should never destroy another. Bless him, and know that it is possible that he may be fulfilling My purposes for him even though it seems he is hindering your own spiritual expression. I have a unique plan for each life, and as you release to Me your tensions, you can rely on Me to continue My work in each soul and bring it ultimately to perfection.

What tensions should I release to God?

Heaven's Gift

from *On the Highroad of Surrender*

My people will dwell in a peaceful habitation,
in secure dwellings, and in quiet resting places.
ISAIAH 32:18 NKJV

—————— ⟨⟨⟩⟩ ——————

Quietness of soul, My child, is heaven's rarest gift enjoyed aforetime. It is unknown to the sinner, for there is no peace to the wicked, but only stress and restlessness. To abide in Me is to know release from tensions; and the ear that is attuned to My voice does not respond to chaos.

People assault their ears with noise to drown the cry of their souls for help. All too often they choose to perpetuate their own misery rather than repent of their evil ways and accept the rulership of another who is greater than themselves.

How well do I abide in God's peace?

The Call of Love

from Come Away My Beloved

Wisdom and knowledge will be the stability of
your times, and the strength of salvation.

ISAIAH 33:6 NKJV

O My beloved, abide under the
shelter of the lattice for I have
betrothed you to Myself, and though
you are sometimes indifferent toward
Me, My love for you is at all times as
a flame of fire. My ardor never cools.
My longing for your love and affection
is deep and constant.

Tarry not for an opportunity to
have more time to be alone with Me.
Take it, though you leave the tasks at
hand. Nothing will suffer. Things are
of less importance than you think.
Our time together is like a garden full
of flowers, whereas the time you give
to things is as a field full of stubble.

*Am I growing a garden or creating a
stubble-filled field?*

Ask!

from *Come Away My Beloved*

The parched ground shall become a pool,
And the thirsty land springs of water.

ISAIAH 35:7 NKJV

If there is dryness within your soul and you do not have this life flowing forth, you need not grieve or chide yourself for being empty. Fill up the empty place with praise. Through praise you may open the gates to your soul's temple. The King will enter and bring His glory

For the promise of the Father is the gift of the indwelling presence of My Holy Spirit, promised to all who have been baptized in the name of Jesus Christ, who have repented of their sins and received remission (see Acts 2:38).

Yes, I say to you, it is a gift. It is written: "How much more will your heavenly Father give the Holy Spirit to those who ask Him" (Luke 11:13 NKJV)! Ask, and you shall receive, and your joy shall be full.

Have I received God's gift of His Spirit?

Do Not Lie Dormant

from *Come Away My Beloved*

But those who wait on the Lord
Shall renew their strength;
They shall mount up with wings like eagles,
They shall run and not be weary,
They shall walk and not faint.

ISAIAH 40:31 NKJV

My child, I need you. Without your active help, I am hampered in My work. You cannot lie idle without hindering the ministry of the Church as a corporate body. You cannot move independently of My Spirit without causing damage to the harmonious working of the whole; for by My Spirit is oneness of thought and action produced. Never be dormant. Do not be slothful, neither let yourself fall asleep.

I am with you, and I will help you. Do not become discouraged or weary or fainthearted, and you will reap My rewards.

Am I discouraged and weary, or waiting on the Lord?

Rivers of Living Water

from *Come Away My Beloved*

The poor and needy seek water. . .
Their tongues fail for thirst.
I, the Lord, will hear them;
I. . .will not forsake them.
I will open rivers in desolate heights,
And fountains in the midst of the valleys;
I will make the wilderness a pool of water,
And the dry land springs of water.

ISAIAH 41:17–18 NKJV

Behold, you are in the hollow of My hand. In the moment that you lift your voice to cry out to Me, then shall My glory gather you up. Yes, I shall wrap you in the garments of joy, and My presence shall be your great reward.

Lift your eyes to Mine. You shall know without a doubt that I love you. Lift your voice to Me in praise; in this way a fountain shall be opened within you, and you will drink of its refreshing waters.

When have I drunk from God's fountain?

Stay Beneath My Wing

from Come Away My Beloved

When you pass through the waters, I will be with
you; and through the rivers, they shall not overflow
you. When you walk through the fire, you shall not
be burned, nor shall the flame scorch you.

Isaiah 43:2 nkjv

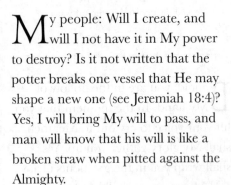

My people: Will I create, and will I not have it in My power to destroy? Is it not written that the potter breaks one vessel that He may shape a new one (see Jeremiah 18:4)? Yes, I will bring My will to pass, and man will know that his will is like a broken straw when pitted against the Almighty.

But My people will know the protection of their God. If I removed you from the scene, you would have no testimony of My miraculous delivering power. Stay beneath My wings, and I will make you a tower of strength to which the fearful may run and find safety.

Am I a strong tower for God?

Why Do You Falter?

from *Progress of Another Pilgrim*

I will go before thee, and make the crooked
places straight.

ISAIAH 45:2

O My child, I have need of you.
Have I not called you and
blessed you? Have I not laid My hand
upon you and shaped you for My purposes? Why, then, do you doubt?

It is only patterns of the past that
bind your thoughts. They can exert no
power over tomorrow except as you
deliberately give them life. With every
task I assign, I also give the enablement.

I have tested your faith many times,
and I know it is strong. Why do you
falter? Rise, and go in My Name,
knowing it is I who thrust you forth. It
is not man. This is My plan for you.
The way should be easy when you
know this.

*What is God's testing accomplishing
in my life?*

Submission and Redemption

from *Progress of Another Pilgrim*

Behold, I have refined thee, but not with silver;
I have chosen thee in the furnace of affliction.

ISAIAH 48:10

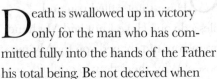

Death is swallowed up in victory only for the man who has committed fully into the hands of the Father his total being. Be not deceived when confronted by the darkness. Out of the hour of temptation comes the light of My transforming work in your soul.

You have asked to be freed of sin and drawn closer to Me. Trust Me now, as I do My perfecting work.

Lean upon My heart. I take no pleasure in afflicting your soul. I desire always for you a speedy deliverance. You help to bring it as you trust Me and as you yield your soul to whatever instrument I use for the accomplishment of My work in you (Romans 7:24–25).

How much have I yielded my heart to God's work?

Preparation

from *Progress of Another Pilgrim*

Thus saith the LORD. . .I am the LORD thy God
which teacheth thee to profit, which leadeth thee
by the way that thou shouldest go.

ISAIAH 48:17

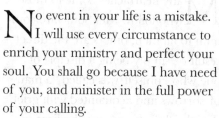

No event in your life is a mistake. I will use every circumstance to enrich your ministry and perfect your soul. You shall go because I have need of you, and minister in the full power of your calling.

You shall go not by man's bidding, but I shall thrust you forth. Be not surprised, neither question how it shall come to pass. The opening of doors is My responsibility; but the preparation of your soul is your own responsibility.

If you would be ready when the time comes, be diligent and follow My guidance in every detail. You are not pampering the flesh but strengthening the body that it may be an adequate vehicle to carry the Spirit.

Am I an adequate vehicle for His Spirit?

The Heavenly Quest

from *Make Haste My Beloved*

He is despised and rejected of men;
a man of sorrows and acquainted with grief.

ISAIAH 53:3

Many heartaches come to those who follow Me. Some are common to all men; others are the direct result of simply being a disciple of one who Himself was called "a man of sorrows and acquainted with grief" (Isaiah 53:3). If you are obedient to Me, you will experience a similar kind of suffering, the suffering of spiritual sacrifice. It is not self-sacrifice, for it is not a giving of self, per se. It is a new and more stringent kind of dedication—it is the heavenly quest for total abandonment to the will of God.

Have I truly abandoned myself to God?

The Glory Life

from Dialogues with God

For my thoughts are not your thoughts, neither are
your ways my ways, saith the LORD.

ISAIAH 55:8

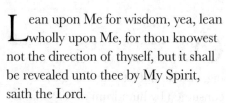

Lean upon Me for wisdom, yea, lean wholly upon Me, for thou knowest not the direction of thyself, but it shall be revealed unto thee by My Spirit, saith the Lord.

Day by day and step by step, thou shalt walk by faith, not by thine own cunningly devised plans.

I desire to do a new thing. How canst thou discover it?

If thou couldst, thou wouldst spoil the thrill of it, as a child finding his gift before the time.

Question Me not, nor ask Me why, neither put confidence in the wisdom of thine own thoughts.

I will never fail thee nor lead thee astray.

I will accomplish that which I purpose.

Am I leaning on God's wisdom or seeking my own?

I Will Use but Not Destroy You

from *Come Away My Beloved*

So shall My word be that goes forth from My
mouth; It shall not return to Me void.

ISAIAH 55:11 NKJV

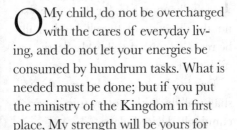

O My child, do not be overcharged
with the cares of everyday living, and do not let your energies be
consumed by humdrum tasks. What is
needed must be done; but if you put
the ministry of the Kingdom in first
place, My strength will be yours for
other tasks, and time will be given to
you for both.

You do not need to respond to every
call. Learn to discern when I would use
you, and when I would have the other
individual lean wholly upon Me.

I will use you, but I will not destroy
you in the using. But you may destroy
yourself if you lack this discernment
and fail to know when to direct others
to look to Me.

*What daily cares have taken my eyes
off the Lord?*

I Do Not Send Storms

from *Progress of Another Pilgrim*

There is no peace, saith my God, to the wicked.

ISAIAH 57:21

Dear Jesus, in the hollow of Thy hand there is peace.

Yes, My child, but do not ask Me to give you peace when you have removed yourself from My hand or if you are unwilling to rest quietly there. I give My peace to all who love and serve Me with singleness of heart. Any duplicity either in character or in aim shall bring disquiet.

I do not *send* storms upon your soul. They are generated by the pressures of your disobedience.

Only in repentance shall my people find peace, and only in singleness of heart shall they find joy.

Am I in a place where God can give me peace?

A Garden of Fountains

from *Come Away My Beloved*

The Lord will guide you continually, And satisfy
your soul in drought, And strengthen your bones;
You shall be like a watered garden, And like a
spring of water, whose waters do not fail.

ISAIAH 58:11 NKJV

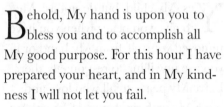

Behold, My hand is upon you to bless you and to accomplish all My good purpose. For this hour I have prepared your heart, and in My kindness I will not let you fail.

Only relinquish all things into My hands; for I can work freely only as you release Me by complete committal—both of yourself and others. As was written of old: "Commit your way to the LORD, trust also in Him, and He shall bring it to pass" (Psalm 37:5 NKJV). I will be your sustaining strength; and My peace shall garrison your mind. Only trust Me—all I do is done in love.

What do I need to relinquish to God?

A Devouring Fire

from *On the Highroad of Surrender*

When the enemy comes in like a flood, the Spirit
of the LORD will lift up a standard against him.

ISAIAH 59:19 NKJV

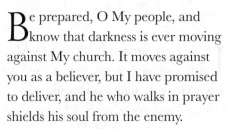

Be prepared, O My people, and know that darkness is ever moving against My church. It moves against you as a believer, but I have promised to deliver, and he who walks in prayer shields his soul from the enemy.

Hold forth the word of truth, both receiving it and giving it, for it is a devouring fire as it goes forth against evil. Lo, it is written, that when I come, I shall destroy the wicked with the words of My mouth (Revelation 19:15, Hebrews 4:12). You shall be able to scatter much darkness and combat the powers of evil as you speak My Word in faith.

How prepared am I to face the darkness?

April 3

Cleanse the Sanctuary

from *Come Away My Beloved*

For My people have committed two evils: They
have forsaken Me, the fountain of living waters,
And hewn themselves cisterns—broken cisterns
that can hold no water.

JEREMIAH 2:13 NKJV

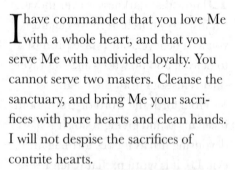

I have commanded that you love Me
with a whole heart, and that you
serve Me with undivided loyalty. You
cannot serve two masters. Cleanse the
sanctuary, and bring Me your sacrifices with pure hearts and clean hands.
I will not despise the sacrifices of
contrite hearts.

I long after you with a love that em-
braces Eternity. Though you go astray,
I will surely draw you back. When
you turn to Me, I shall bridge the gap.
Although you have strayed, I have not
left you. Wherever you turn to Me in
love and confession, I am there in the
midst of you.

Do I love God with a whole heart?

The Armor of Light

from Progress of Another Pilgrim

O LORD, I know that the way of man is not in
himself: it is not in man that walketh
to direct his steps.
JEREMIAH 10:23

O My child, I call you to surrender.
No problem confronts you that
I cannot resolve. Given the opportunity, I will spare you disappointment and regret. Confess, and I will
forgive, and I will extricate you from
this situation that you have brought
upon yourself.

You ran ahead of Me and fell into
a snare. I will go with you Myself and
make the crooked places straight and we
will go on again, together. This time you
will wait for My leading.

Wear the armor of the Spirit, and
you have My protection. Fear not what
others can do to harm you. Fear only
your own tendency to act independently.

*In what ways do I tend to act
independently of God?*

To Feel Need Is to Receive Grace

from *Make Haste, My Beloved*

Call unto Me, and I will answer thee,
and show thee great and mighty things,
which thou knowest not.

JEREMIAH 33:3

My mercy flows in the stream of all your woes, My child. No obstacle within yourself can restrict My grace. I use many vessels while they are struggling with their failures; for in their conscious sense of need, they are more yielded to Me than they who think themselves to be without flaw. Nothing restricts the Spirit's work more than the smug satisfaction of the spiritually proud.

To feel need is to receive grace. The mighty things which you do not comprehend are the miraculous things I do for you and through you in your acknowledged times of need. I act in and through you according to My grace and My own ability.

Do I feel the need for His grace?

Be Thou My Door
of Hope

from *On the Highroad of Surrender*

It is of the LORD's mercies that we are
not consumed, because his compassions fail not.
They are new every morning:
great is thy faithfulness.
LAMENTATIONS 3:22–23

———

Out of the depths you have cried unto Me. I am gracious and full of compassion. My heart is touched by the feeling of your infirmities, and I am acquainted with your grief (Hebrews 4:15).

I am your help, for to whom else shall you go? I will be your Door of Hope, though darkness is round about you.

Is God my only door of hope?

Eternity and Time

from *Come Away My Beloved*

A wheel in the middle of a wheel.
EZEKIEL 1:16

Behold, a new day is dawning! Do not let the sound of war and discords deafen your ears to My message; for I would speak to you a word of encouragement and would bring you tidings of hope.

My little children, I have not gone away never to return; but I will surely come, yes, even at a time when you least expect.

Do not focus on the problems of the world; but look up, for surely your deliverance is near.

My ageless purposes are set in Eternity. Time is like a little wheel set within the big wheel of Eternity. The little wheel turns swiftly and shall one day cease. The big wheel turns not, but goes straightforward. Time is your responsibility—Eternity is Mine!

How well do I keep eternity in mind as I spend my earthly time?

I Will Share My Secrets

from *Make Haste My Beloved*

He revealeth the deep and secret things:
he knoweth what is in the darkness,
and the light dwelleth with him.

DANIEL 2:22

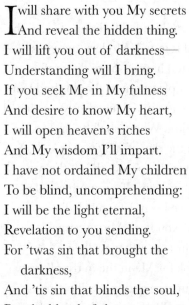

I will share with you My secrets
And reveal the hidden thing.
I will lift you out of darkness—
Understanding will I bring.
If you seek Me in My fulness
And desire to know My heart,
I will open heaven's riches
And My wisdom I'll impart.
I have not ordained My children
To be blind, uncomprehending:
I will be the light eternal,
Revelation to you sending.
For 'twas sin that brought the
    darkness,
And 'tis sin that blinds the soul,
But the blood of the atonement
Opens eyes and makes men whole.

*What secrets has God been sharing
with me?*

In the Fiery Furnace

from *Progress of Another Pilgrim*

He answered and said, Lo, I see four men loose,
walking in the midst of the fire, and they have no
hurt; and the form of the fourth is like the
Son of God.

DANIEL 3:25

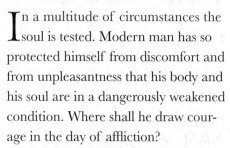

In a multitude of circumstances the soul is tested. Modern man has so protected himself from discomfort and from unpleasantness that his body and his soul are in a dangerously weakened condition. Where shall he draw courage in the day of affliction?

Never try to smooth out the way for either yourself or another unless you have been definitely led to do so. Always you need My guidance, even for your acts of benevolence.

Look for Me in the midst of every fiery furnace and you will be influenced by My Spirit rather than by your own natural impulses (2 Corinthians 11:16–32; 2 Timothy 2:3).

Where do I look when I face the furnace?

The Coward Seeks Release

from *On the Highroad of Surrender*

And the princes, governors, and captains, and the
king's counsellors, being gathered together, saw
these men, upon whose bodies the fire had no
power, nor was an hair of their head singed, neither
were their coats changed, nor the smell of fire had
passed on them.

DANIEL 3:27

Hold fast, My child, for in the hour of anguish, then shall you walk in victory. Do not pray to be brought out of the fire until after you have found Me real in the midst of it.

The coward seeks release from pressure. The courageous pray for strength to overcome the evil force.

What am I praying for today?

April 11

Liberty

from On the Highroad of Surrender

All of whose works are truth, and His ways justice.
And those who walk in pride He is able to put down.
DANIEL 4:37 NKJV

———— ❦ ————

Stand fast in the liberty wherein I
have made you free and allow no
one to move you into a position of
compromise. Be diligent to make the
most of the opportunities thus afforded
you, and do not miss any.

You will never discover what I have
planned for you if in your zeal you run
ahead and become again entangled.
I free you and I want keep you free.
Why do you look to others for help
when I am already at work moving
mountains, opening doors and touching hearts on your behalf?

Be at peace.

How free is my life?

Faith Manifesting in Divine Response

from Progress of Another Pilgrim

My God hath sent his angel, and hath shut the lions'
mouths, that they have not hurt me: forasmuch as
before him innocency was found in me; and also
before thee, O king, have I done no hurt.

DANIEL 6:22

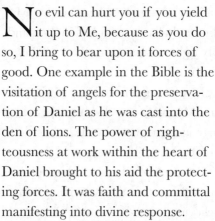

No evil can hurt you if you yield it up to Me, because as you do so, I bring to bear upon it forces of good. One example in the Bible is the visitation of angels for the preservation of Daniel as he was cast into the den of lions. The power of righteousness at work within the heart of Daniel brought to his aid the protecting forces. It was faith and committal manifesting into divine response.

The same law will work for you. Test it and prove it. You will find that your fear of calamity will gradually be dissolved, and you will gain a firmer inner confidence.

How can I yield evil up to God?

A Yielded, Believing Vessel

from *Come Away My Beloved*

But the people who know their God shall be
strong, and carry out great exploits.

DANIEL 11:32 NKJV

Mine is the wisdom and the honor and the power and the glory and shall be so forever and ever. I make the nations rise and kingdoms fall, but My throne shall be established in Zion and My righteousness throughout all the earth.

I am never defeated, but My justice and My mercy are obstructed by human ignorance and by the lack of faith in even My children.

Be aware of Me. I can accomplish great things through even one yielded, believing vessel. Remember David, and how I wrought a great victory for the armies of Israel through his courage when all others were paralyzed by fear.

Move on, and never entertain the thought of retreat.

Where am I moving for God?

Comfort in Affliction

from *Come Away My Beloved*

Then they will seek My face;
In their affliction they will earnestly seek Me.
HOSEA 5:15 NKJV

O My people, has not My hand fashioned for you many signs and wonders? Have I not ministered to you in miraculous ways? How is it you say therefore in your heart, "I will turn again to human strength"? Will you not, then, trust Me now in this new emergency, even as you have trusted Me in the past?

Lean hard upon Me, for I bring you through to new victories, and restoration shall follow what seems now to be a wind of destruction. Draw upon the resources of My grace. Heaven rejoices when you go through trials with a singing spirit.

Be like a beacon light. His own glorious radiance shall shine through you, and Christ Himself will be revealed.

What kind of beacon am I for my Savior?

Grace

from *Progress of Another Pilgrim*

Then shall we know, if we follow on to know the
LORD: his going forth is prepared as the morning;
and he shall come unto us as the rain, as the latter
and former rain unto the earth.

HOSEA 6:3

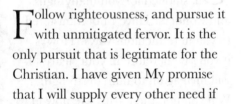

F ollow righteousness, and pursue it
with unmitigated fervor. It is the
only pursuit that is legitimate for the
Christian. I have given My promise
that I will supply every other need if
you seek righteousness. It is in the self-
less abandon to the Spirit that grace is
nurtured.

I have freely extended My grace
to you. Now I desire to see My grace
developed in you!

*How is God's grace being
developed in me?*

Sound the Trumpet

from On the Highroad of Surrender

Blow the trumpet in Zion, and sound an alarm in
My holy mountain! Let all the inhabitants of the
land tremble: for the day of the LORD is coming,
for it is at hand.

JOEL 2:1 NKJV

Be alert. Be vigilant. Sound the
alarm from My holy mountain.
Challenge my people that they be not
overtaken by the enemy because they
have a false sense of security. By My
Spirit you shall overcome, and by My
Word you shall prevail.

Gird on the armor of My holiness,
and speak the word of faith. Fear not
the enemy; for he has already been
stripped of his power, and victory is
yours. Surely I will send My delivering angel to stand beside you, and you
shall not turn back, neither give in to
weariness, for the Lord your God, He
is your strength, and in His hand is the
reward.

How alert and vigilant am I?

April 17

The Harvest Is Overripe

from *Progress of Another Pilgrim*

Put ye in the sickle, for the harvest is ripe: come, get
you down; for the press is full, the fats overflow; for
their wickedness is great.

JOEL 3:13

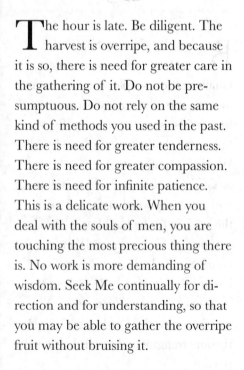

The hour is late. Be diligent. The harvest is overripe, and because it is so, there is need for greater care in the gathering of it. Do not be presumptuous. Do not rely on the same kind of methods you used in the past. There is need for greater tenderness. There is need for greater compassion. There is need for infinite patience. This is a delicate work. When you deal with the souls of men, you are touching the most precious thing there is. No work is more demanding of wisdom. Seek Me continually for direction and for understanding, so that you may be able to gather the overripe fruit without bruising it.

*What can I do to help harvest
the fruit of souls?*

The Golden Path

from *Progress of Another Pilgrim*

Surely the Lord GOD will do nothing, but he
revealeth his secret unto his servants the prophets.

AMOS 3:7

O My child, I have a special path
for you. Search it out diligently.
Let Me guide you in it. Follow not
other sheep aimlessly as they roam
through My pastures. Lo, I call you to
follow me.

I have you on a path which is all
your own. It is not My way for anybody else. It will become clear to you
only by revelation. This can only come
from Me.

I call it the golden path. It is the
golden path for you. It is a sacred
secret between us. Guard it and keep
it, and treasure it in the secret places
of your soul.

*Am I walking on God's golden path
for me?*

April 19

These Are Days of the Moving of My Spirit

from *Come Away My Beloved*

"Behold, the days are coming," says the Lord GOD,
"That I will send a famine on the land, not a famine of bread, nor a thirst for water, but of hearing
the words of the LORD."

AMOS 8:11 NKJV

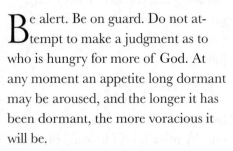

Be alert. Be on guard. Do not attempt to make a judgment as to
who is hungry for more of God. At
any moment an appetite long dormant
may be aroused, and the longer it has
been dormant, the more voracious it
will be.

Give My Word—These are the
days of the moving of My Spirit; will
you resist if I wish to make you My
aqueduct?

Stay clear—allow no constriction
nor obstruction, and do not be stingy.
Growth will spring forth wherever the
waters reach.

What obstructions may be blocking the
Spirit's flow in my life?

Gentleness

from *Progress of Another Pilgrim*

He hath shewed thee, O man, what is good; and
what doth the LORD require of thee, but to do
justly, and to love mercy, and to walk humbly
with thy God?

MICAH 6:8

B e obedient to My commands: so
shall I bless you. Let Me guide
you: thus shall you know the right
path. Follow always the call of the
Spirit. All who listen shall hear. Move
with the flexibility of a yielded will.
Mercies are laid up in store for the
humble.

Gentleness of spirit brings overcoming power. It is not the strong will,
but the yielded will that is blessed in
My sight.

*How much am I yielding my will
to God?*

April 21

New Songs in Your Mouth

from *Come Away My Beloved*

But unto you that fear my name shall the Sun of
righteousness arise with healing in his wings; and
ye shall go forth, and grow up as calves of the stall.

MALACHI 4:2

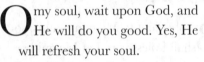

O my soul, wait upon God, and He will do you good. Yes, He will refresh your soul.

For His tender mercies are never failing, and His kindness toward you is as the morning. As the Sun of Righteousness shall arise with healing in His wings (see Malachi 4:2), so shall your God be unto you.

For the night is past; yes, I bring you into a new place: a place of rejoicing in Me such as you have not known as yet.

For I shall fill your soul with fatness, and I will be with you to do you good.

What am I rejoicing about today?

The Attribute of Mercy

from *Progress of Another Pilgrim*

Blessed are the merciful: for they shall obtain mercy.

MATTHEW 5:7

Mercy is one of My attributes which I strongly desire you to have.

If you are not merciful, it would have been better had you not presumed to become My disciple. Without this quality in ministry, there can be no genuine blessing flowing through your life. In each relationship with others, if you do not have mercy, you will blight, not bless.

Without mercy, Calvary would have become a preachment of condemnation rather than of forgiveness. Expressing, as He did, His mercy toward His enemies, He provided you an example of the extent to which your own compassion should operate. You may never achieve an expression of love in the same degree, but let it be always the measure and the guide by which you judge your own attitudes.

In what ways can I show more mercy?

The Blessings of the Pure in Heart

from *Come Away My Beloved*

Blessed are the pure in heart:
for they shall see God.

MATTHEW 5:8

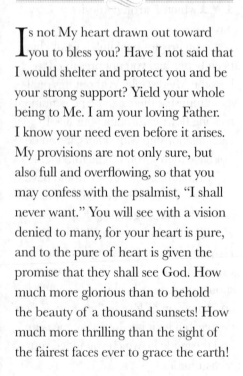

Is not My heart drawn out toward you to bless you? Have I not said that I would shelter and protect you and be your strong support? Yield your whole being to Me. I am your loving Father. I know your need even before it arises. My provisions are not only sure, but also full and overflowing, so that you may confess with the psalmist, "I shall never want." You will see with a vision denied to many, for your heart is pure, and to the pure of heart is given the promise that they shall see God. How much more glorious than to behold the beauty of a thousand sunsets! How much more thrilling than the sight of the fairest faces ever to grace the earth!

Do I delight in the thought of seeing God?

Chastening

from *Come Away My Beloved*

Ye are the salt of the earth: but if the salt have
lost his savour, wherewith shall it be salted? it is
thenceforth good for nothing, but to be cast out,
and to be trodden under foot of men.

MATTHEW 5:13

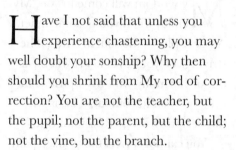

Have I not said that unless you
experience chastening, you may
well doubt your sonship? Why then
should you shrink from My rod of correction? You are not the teacher, but
the pupil; not the parent, but the child;
not the vine, but the branch.

Discipline and correction must
come if you desire to be brought into
conformity to My divine will. Shun
nothing My hand brings to bear upon
your life. Accept My blessings and My
comfort, but do not despise My stern
dealings. All are working toward your
ultimate perfection.

In what ways has God been chastening me?

On Not Resisting Evil

from *On the Highroad of Surrender*

But I say unto you, That ye resist not evil:
but whosoever shall smite thee on thy right cheek,
turn to him the other also.

MATTHEW 5:39

My wisdom will come to you, My child, when you become quiet. Anxiety places the soul in stress. The strivings of your own heart will be as out of harmony with My Spirit as the evil you wish to combat. This is why the Scripture says, "Resist not evil."

You cannot correct the crooked path of another, but you can let Me show you how to make a straight path of your own. Never fear the darkness. . .avoid it.

Do not use your energy destroying the house of your enemy. If it is an unsound structure, it will eventually fall. You need your full attention to build rightly your own.

How often am I quiet before the Lord?

Come into the Secret
Chambers of Communion

from *Come Away My Beloved*

Pray to thy Father which is in secret; and thy Father
which seeth in secret shall reward thee openly.

MATTHEW 6:6

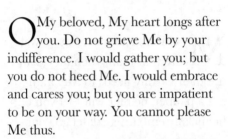

O My beloved, My heart longs after
you. Do not grieve Me by your
indifference. I would gather you; but
you do not heed Me. I would embrace
and caress you; but you are impatient
to be on your way. You cannot please
Me thus.

I have called you to come into the
secret chambers of solitary communion. They are dark; but the comfort
of My Person is there. Out of darkness
comes great treasure.

The dazzle and glitter of public life
is attractive to the natural eye; but I
would closet you in the secret places of
humility and discipline of soul, denying
the things that pertain to the outward
man in order to perfect the inner life
and enrich your knowledge of Myself.

*What has God shown me in His secret
chamber?*

Take No Thought for Tomorrow

from *Progress of Another Pilgrim*

Consider the lilies of the field. . .they toil not,
neither do they spin: and yet. . .even Solomon in all
his glory was not arrayed like one of these.

MATTHEW 6:28–29

My children are never more well cared for than when they commit their earthly needs to Me. I am not a pauper, neither will I let you be financially embarrassed; let go your earthly cares.

I do not forbid you to work, only to worry. The best way to break the power of worry is to refuse to take thought for tomorrow. Today is rarely a problem. Most anxious thoughts are related to the future. Put all of tomorrow into My keeping.

For today you need Wisdom. For tomorrow you need Faith. Try it, and you will never want to go back to the old way.

Worry or faith—which do I have?

Resignation

from Come Away My Beloved

Seek ye first the kingdom of God and His righteousness, and all these things shall be added unto you.

Matthew 6:33

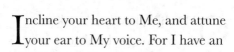

Incline your heart to Me, and attune your ear to My voice. For I have an urgent message to give you.

Do not set out to establish your own designs. I have already set in motion My divine will and purpose, and I would not have you interfere. I am jealous of My children: they are Mine, and you shall not intrude in any way to hinder My plans from working out. Yes, you may do many things, but only that which I direct you to do can have My blessing.

Resign all into My hands—your loved ones as well as your own self. Be obedient to the still, small voice. Fret not about carnal things, but concern your-self first and always with spiritual values.

What am I seeking first?

April 29

One Day at a Time

from *Come Away My Beloved*

Therefore do not worry about tomorrow, for
tomorrow will worry about its own things. Sufficient
for the day is its own trouble.

MATTHEW 6:34 NKJV

O My child, have you not known
the way of the Lord, and can
you not trust Him now? Nothing shall
befall you but that which comes from
His hand. No one shall set upon you
to hurt you, for your God has built
around you a wall of fire.

Be content with what each day
brings, rejoicing in your God, for
surely He shall deliver you. He is the
One who has brought you here.

His way is discernable to the eye of
faith. His heart is surely your strong
tower. In His affection you have security. In His love are your hope and
your peace.

*How content am I with what
each day brings?*

The Road Is Steep

from Come Away My Beloved

Narrow is the gate and difficult is the way which
leads to life, and there are few who find it.

MATTHEW 7:14 NKJV

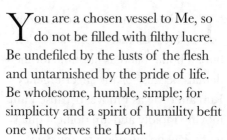

You are a chosen vessel to Me, so
do not be filled with filthy lucre.
Be undefiled by the lusts of the flesh
and untarnished by the pride of life.
Be wholesome, humble, simple; for
simplicity and a spirit of humility befit
one who serves the Lord.

Pride lifts up. It exalts self rather
than Christ. Humility brings down to
the level of service, and you are not to
be worshiped, but to serve.

You are My treasure. I delight in
you when you are fully yielded to Me
with no thoughts of personal ambition
or achievement. If you wish for anything, wish for more of My nearness.
If you long after anything, long after
more of My righteousness and more
of My love.

Am I wholesome, humble, and simple—
or prideful?

Break Old Patterns

from *Progress of Another Pilgrim*

But Jesus said unto him, Follow me;
and let the dead bury their dead.
MATTHEW 8:22

The time is now because the hour is late; yes, there is not a day left, but an hour. There is not time for incidentals because of the sheer urgency. Run after Me as I move, because I am moving rapidly and am doing a quick work. Pay no attention to any voice except the voice of the Spirit. Let no one use you except the Father. Believe no one except the Son. Live in expectancy and move in absolute obedience.

Break out of old patterns, and make no provision for your own personal wishes. Purify your desires so that you do not stand in your own way.

Am I running after Jesus or the world?

Faith and Action

from *Come Away My Beloved*

According to your faith be it unto you.

MATTHEW 9:29

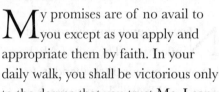

My promises are of no avail to you except as you apply and appropriate them by faith. In your daily walk, you shall be victorious only to the degree that you trust Me. I can help you only as you ask. I will meet you at every point where you put action alongside your prayers.

Overburdened as the world is with trouble and sickness, I need those who have proved My sufficiency in personal experience to lead the suffering to the fountains of life.

Never begrudge time given to chronic complainers, but recognize in each encounter the opportunity to speak a word that may lead to their liberation. No case is too hard for Me.

How has my life proved Jesus' sufficiency?

I Am Everywhere

from *Progress of Another Pilgrim*

Heal the sick, cleanse the lepers, raise the dead, cast
out devils: freely ye have received, freely give.

MATTHEW 10:8

Never flounder on the rocks of indecision. The call of My heart to you is for your utter abandon to the waters of My will. I am everywhere. Think not that any man can shut Me out. Wherever you go you bear the Wind of the Spirit. It shall bring new life into any situation. It shall breathe upon the dead, and they shall live. It shall touch the one who has completely given up with a ray of new courage, so that though he may have lost all hope he shall be lifted out of the place of despondency into My loving arms and into an atmosphere of faith once again.

How is the "Wind of the Spirit" working through me?

Thy God Forever

from Dialogues with God

But the very hairs of your head are all
numbered.
MATTHEW 10:30

Behold, I am Thy God forever.
I am with thee. In the time of
trouble, I will be thy strong defense,
and in the hour of need, I am thy sure
habitation.

Mine eye is ever watchful and I
shall undertake for thee according to
My glorious riches. Is it not written:
"the very hairs of your head are all
numbered" (Matthew 10:30)? Surely
My love for thee is altered by no external circumstances.

I am the Lord thy God that
changeth not, neither grows weary nor
irritable. My love is constant. Hold to
this one thing as the needle holds to
the pole.

I shall not disappoint thee in any way.

Am I holding fast to God alone?

The Spiritual Realm

from *On the Highroad of Surrender*

Come to Me, all you who labor and are heavy
laden, and I will give you rest. Take My yoke upon
you and learn from Me, for I am gentle and lowly
in heart, and you will find rest for your souls.
MATTHEW 11:28–29 NKJV

Do not be concerned about failing
people. Your only true concern
should be that you not fail Me. I am
making last-minute preparations for
My soon-coming. The table is already
spread for the marriage supper for the
Lamb. Do not frustrate My plans for
you by pursuing your own.

I want you walking and expressing
in the spiritual realm. For this purpose
have I painstakingly prepared your
soul. Cast aside your carnal reasoning.
Cast aside even your consideration for
people and the threat of disappointing
them. Would you rather that I be disappointed, in preference to others? Can
you not trust Me? Would I fail anyone?

Who am I most concerned about serving?

Release Your Grief

from Come Away My Beloved

Take My yoke upon you and learn from Me, for I
am gentle and lowly in heart, and you will find rest
for your souls.

MATTHEW 11:29 NKJV

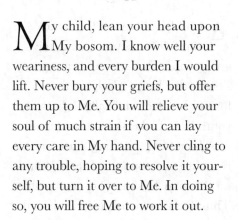

My child, lean your head upon
My bosom. I know well your
weariness, and every burden I would
lift. Never bury your griefs, but offer
them up to Me. You will relieve your
soul of much strain if you can lay
every care in My hand. Never cling to
any trouble, hoping to resolve it yourself, but turn it over to Me. In doing
so, you will free Me to work it out.

*What personal grief can I place
in Jesus' hands?*

Avoid Frivolity

from *Progress of Another Pilgrim*

But I say unto you, That every idle word that men
shall speak, they shall give account thereof
in the day of judgment.

MATTHEW 12:36

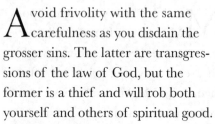

A void frivolity with the same
carefulness as you disdain the
grosser sins. The latter are transgres-
sions of the law of God, but the
former is a thief and will rob both
yourself and others of spiritual good.

A bantering spirit may cause you to
be oblivious to opportunities to minister that may lie directly in your path.
Thus if you are indulging in spiritual
profligacy, you rob the other person
of the blessing you could have given,
and you rob yourself of the reward
you would have received had you been
walking softly in the Spirit.

What must I do to avoid frivolity?

Guard Against
Foolishness

from *Progress of Another Pilgrim*

For by thy words thou shalt be justified, and by thy
words thou shalt be condemned.

MATTHEW 12:37

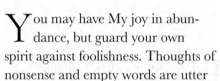

Y ou may have My joy in abundance, but guard your own
spirit against foolishness. Thoughts of
nonsense and empty words are utter
waste. I can use them in no way at all.

All words are either actively good
or actively negative, and if they are
negative, they are destructive. They will
nullify the testimony I would establish
when you speak My words, so that if
you mix the two, the good will be can-
celled out by the evil.

You cannot afford such carelessness.
My servants must be wise as serpents
and blameless as doves. Let your every
word be full of grace and taste of the
saltiness of divine goodness. Let it be
known of you by your good conversation that you have been much with Me.

What guards against foolishness can
I establish?

On Coping with Success

from *On the Highroad of Surrender*

Because it has been given to you to know the
mysteries of the kingdom of heaven, but to them
it has not been given. For whoever has, to him
more will be given, and he will have abundance;
but whoever does not have, even what he has will
be taken away from him.

MATTHEW 13:11–12 NKJV

Be never entangled by thoughts
concerning the reactions of others
to your ministry. No decision should
ever be made on this basis. Minister,
and follow the leading of the Spirit.
Search your heart, and pray for the
strength to receive great results.

I may withhold blessings because
in My love and wisdom I foresee your
own unreadiness to receive. Learn
how to prepare your mind and heart
to cope with success, otherwise when it
comes you may by your very unreadiness and lack of fortitude undo the
good that has been done.

*How concerned am I about other
people's approval?*

Angels Are Separating

from *Progress of Another Pilgrim*

The harvest is the end of the world;
and the reapers are the angels.

MATTHEW 13:39

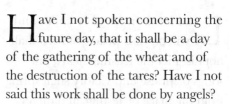

Have I not spoken concerning the future day, that it shall be a day of the gathering of the wheat and of the destruction of the tares? Have I not said this work shall be done by angels?

You have been aware of the presence and ministry of angels. You, as believers, are being gathered unto the Father. Meanwhile the children of wrath and disobedience are being separated and gathered to each other.

Truly, angels are separating. Know this when you would wonder why one is brought in and another goes out into the night, never to return. Question it not, for you are seeing this prophecy fulfilled, at least in part. It shall be accelerated as the end draws nearer.

You shall find in this understanding much peace of heart.

What is my part in the harvest?

Faith Released

from On the Highroad of Surrender

For whoever desires to save his life will lose it, but
whoever loses his life for My sake will find it.

MATTHEW 16:25 NKJV

Lean hard on Me, My child, and I will be your peace. Storms shall not disquiet the trusting heart, but songs of praise and victory shall spring from the place of testing, and mercy shall prevail where faith is released, in spite of every contrary wind.

No harm can come to the one who looks to Me as his protection, but he who endeavors to protect himself shall be exposed to the destructive forces he seeks to escape.

He shall not know peace who runs after the rewards of the world.

Where do I turn for protection?

Outflow

from *On the Highroad of Surrender*

For what profit is it to a man if he gains the whole
world, and loses his own soul? Or what will a man
give in exchange for his soul?

MATTHEW 16:26 NKJV

B lessings are released when the soul
is content with nothing of earthly
value. The spirit is prepared for worldly success only after it has learned to
care nothing for it. I fill the hand that
lies open in worship. The hand that
grasps shall be forever empty.

Learn to leave to My love and wisdom all your destiny. Nothing ought
concern you but the health of your
soul and the outflow of your life. You
will free your soul as you refuse to seek
anything and desire only to give. Then
shall I bless you with increase and only
then will it not impoverish your spirit.

How is the outflow of my life?

May 13

Challenge and Growth

from On the Highroad of Surrender

This kind does not go out except by
prayer and fasting.
MATTHEW 17:21 NKJV

In all the challenges of life, My
hand is outstretched to give you
courage. No stress need overwhelm
if your confidence is in Me. To lean
upon the arm of flesh brings certain
disaster.

When the Psalmist penned, "From
the Lord comes my help," he excluded
all other sources. Effective faith is born
of total consecration. My Spirit alone
can bring forth this kind of dedication
and inner strength.

Continual challenges bring constant growth, and when you pray for
respite from the conflict, you rob your
soul and retard its maturation.

Hold before Me at all times a heart
that prefers instruction to comfort.
You cannot have both.

Do I prefer instruction to comfort?

God's Purpose

from *On the Highroad of Surrender*

Now behold, one came and said to Him, "Good
Teacher, what good thing shall I do that I may have
eternal life?" So He said to him, "Why do you call
Me good? No one is good but One, that is, God.
But if you want to enter into life,
keep the commandments."

MATTHEW 19:16–17 NKJV

G od's purpose in making you
holy involves His own glory. He
is not waiting to hear you called holy;
He is listening to hear you call Him
holy. He is not interested in making
you a reputation, but in making you a
disciple.

The rich young ruler flattered Jesus
by addressing him as "good master,"
and Jesus rebuked him, pressing upon
him the necessity to decide either to not
call him good, or to acknowledge His
deity. How then can He be pleased that
one should desire such a reputation?

Am I truly Jesus' disciple?

Love's Servant

from *Make Haste My Beloved*

He that is greatest among you shall be your servant.

MATTHEW 23:11

———————— ⟡ ————————

You seek acceptance, forgetting that Jesus was despised and rejected.

You seek happiness, ignoring the fact that He was a man of sorrows.

You seek security, when the Son of Man had no certain place to lay His head.

Why do you seek falsely? Because you have not learned to love. Love changes all the desires. Love knows that doing the Father's will is the only thing of value. Because love does not seek its own, it is not dismayed when circumstances are unfavorable.

He who has love will labor happily though unremunerated and sacrifice personal comfort without protest or complaint. He will measure happiness by his power to give and weakness by his limitation to bring comfort to those in need.

Love is the source of joy, the touchstone of all meaningful human expression.

How well do I love when circumstances are unfavorable?

The Echo of My Voice

from On the Highroad of Surrender

Woe to you, scribes and Pharisees, hypocrites!
For you cleanse the outside of the cup and dish,
but inside they are full of extortion and
self-indulgence.

MATTHEW 23:25 NKJV

⚬⚬⚬

O My child, the cry of your soul is the echo of My voice calling you to repentance. Your love for Me will place you under My chastening rod, for as long as you love Me, you will seek My face even when you anticipate My reproach. The hand of punishment that restores to fellowship is kinder than the hand of sympathy of the one who would palliate your conscience in an evil action.

Let Me deal with any unsoundness in your spirit, and I will spare you the humiliation of open shame. Inner conviction comes through My Word, and this is your only sure way of finding peace in My presence.

When have I felt God's conviction concerning my deeds?

Responsibilities and Privileges

from *Progress of Another Pilgrim*

For unto every one that hath shall be given, and he
shall have abundance: but from him that hath not
shall be taken away even that which he hath.

MATTHEW 25:29

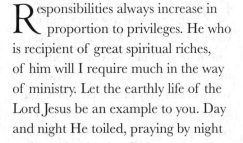

Responsibilities always increase in proportion to privileges. He who is recipient of great spiritual riches, of him will I require much in the way of ministry. Let the earthly life of the Lord Jesus be an example to you. Day and night He toiled, praying by night and working by day. So must you. The present hour is even more critical because the time of final judgment is coming upon mankind. Darkness is deepening, and the light of My witness is more needed than ever before.

Be faithful, and you shall deliver others and preserve your own soul.

*What responsibilities and privileges
has God given me?*

The Broadening View

from Dialogues with God

For there is nothing hid, which shall not be
manifested; neither was any thing kept secret, but
that it should come abroad.

MARK 4:22

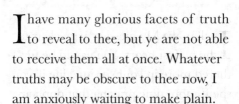

I have many glorious facets of truth to reveal to thee, but ye are not able to receive them all at once. Whatever truths may be obscure to thee now, I am anxiously waiting to make plain.

So give thyself to diligent study— yea, search the Scriptures for they are given for the purpose of revealing Me. It shall be as when one ascends a mountain, and from each successively higher vantage point he thrills at an increasingly broadening view. I will take thee progressively higher via the written Word until that day when ye shall see Me face to face! Then shall ye know Me and understand Me even as I now know you.

What view am I seeing?

The Listening Ear

from On the Highroad of Surrender

If any man have ears to hear, let him hear. And he
said unto them, Take heed what ye hear: with what
measure ye mete, it shall be measured to you: and
unto you that hear shall more be given.

MARK 4:23–24

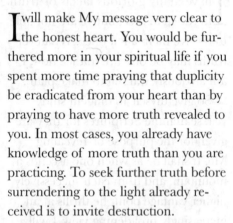

I will make My message very clear to
the honest heart. You would be fur-
thered more in your spiritual life if you
spent more time praying that duplicity
be eradicated from your heart than by
praying to have more truth revealed to
you. In most cases, you already have
knowledge of more truth than you are
practicing. To seek further truth before
surrendering to the light already received is to invite destruction.

My commandments are very precious to those who are desirous of
doing My will. Those who truly wish
to please Me do not seek ways to ratio-
nalize and bypass My laws.

*How does my knowledge compare
with my practice?*

Dismiss with Dispatch

from *Progress of Another Pilgrim*

And when he was come into the ship, he that had
been possessed with the devil prayed him that he
might be with him. Howbeit Jesus suffered him
not, but saith unto him, Go home to thy friends,
and tell them how great things the Lord
hath done for thee.

MARK 5:18–19

Nothing I am doing would seem
strange to you if you had been
more attentive to My voice.

I can lead you only as you wait
upon Me for guidance. Man will
always take you down the wrong path.
It is folly to stumble along in blindness.
I am your friend. Can you not trust
My love? Would I ever harm you? Do
I not give you a full measure of joy?

Do I view Jesus as my friend?

Inner Communion

from *Progress of Another Pilgrim*

And whosoever shall not receive you, nor hear you,
when ye depart thence, shake off the dust under
your feet for a testimony against them.

MARK 6:11

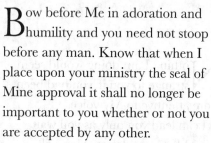

B ow before Me in adoration and
humility and you need not stoop
before any man. Know that when I
place upon your ministry the seal of
Mine approval it shall no longer be
important to you whether or not you
are accepted by any other.

This is an activity in which we are
co-laborers together—I and you and
the Father. Keep a strong awareness
of this identification. You will lose the
anointing if you allow anyone to enter
and distract.

Stay in the holy place of inner communion and I will break forth through
your vessel and manifest My glory
outwardly.

How is my communion with God?

Be My Ally

from *Come Away My Beloved*

And he [Jesus] said unto them, Come ye yourselves
apart into a desert place, and rest a while.

MARK 6:31

My children, do not fear nor resist My voice. When I speak to you, you will know that it is I, the Lord God. As I spoke to Isaiah I will speak to you. Is it not strange that you are astonished at the way I speak to you? Instead, those who do not hear My voice ought to marvel!

Your busyness wearies Me. Small wonder you are yourself fatigued! Your fretfulness grieves Me. I long to take it from you and give you instead the balm of Gilead. Be My ally. I will endow you with life so dynamic that you will serve Me before you have time to even think about putting forth the effort to do so.

*In what areas of my life do I need
His balm today?*

Sacrifice, My Status Symbol

from *Come Away My Beloved*

For whoever desires to save his life will lose it, but whoever loses his life for My sake and the gospel's will save it.

MARK 8:35 NKJV

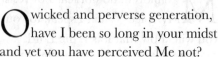

O wicked and perverse generation, have I been so long in your midst and yet you have perceived Me not? Yes, and when I speak to you, you do not hear.

O My children, you behave not as sons and daughters but as strangers. You hold meetings in My Name, and give honor to men, but not to Me. You boast that you serve Me, but in truth you serve your own ego.

You would make Christianity pleasant and acceptable. Your Savior did not find it so. You would make it comfortable and accommodating to your own schedule. He knew nothing of such a false religion.

Do you desire to truly follow Me? Look for the bloodstained prints of My feet.

Who am I really serving today?

Key to Joy

from *On the Highroad of Surrender*

For whoever desires to save his life will lose it, but
whoever loses his life for My sake and the gospel's
will save it. For what will it profit a man if he gains
the whole world, and loses his own soul?

MARK 8:35–36 NKJV

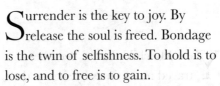

Surrender is the key to joy. By
release the soul is freed. Bondage
is the twin of selfishness. To hold is to
lose, and to free is to gain.

Meditation opens the door to revelation, and revelation brings liberation.
Test it in any given situation. You will
find that you hold in your own hand
the instrument of life. It will work like
a magic eye to open the heaviest door.

Am I in bondage, or have I surrendered?

By Silence Ye Rob Me of My Glory

from *Dialogues with God*

Whosoever therefore shall be ashamed of me and
of my words in this adulterous and sinful generation;
of him also shall the Son of man be ashamed, when
he cometh in the glory of his Father
with the holy angels.

MARK 8:38

Yea, My child, I have been be-
trayed more times by silence than
by words. By words a man may sin
against Me, but by silence do ye rob
Me of My Glory.

Never miss an opportunity to up-
hold Me; and know this: as ye testify
of Me and plead My cause before
men, I will surely plead thy cause and
witness for thee before the Father.

But as it is written: if you are
ashamed of Me before men, I will be
ashamed of you when I stand before
the Father in your behalf (Mark 8:38).

How have I robbed God of His glory?

Perspective and Depth

from Progress of Another Pilgrim

And Peter answered and said to Jesus, Master, it
is good for us to be here: and let us make three
tabernacles; one for thee, and one for Moses, and
one for Elias. For he wist not what to say; for they
were sore afraid.

MARK 9:5–6

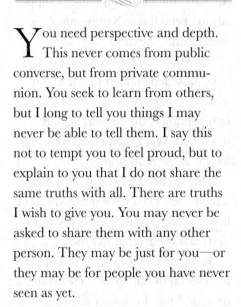

You need perspective and depth.
This never comes from public
converse, but from private communion. You seek to learn from others,
but I long to tell you things I may
never be able to tell them. I say this
not to tempt you to feel proud, but to
explain to you that I do not share the
same truths with all. There are truths
I wish to give you. You may never be
asked to share them with any other
person. They may be just for you—or
they may be for people you have never
seen as yet.

What private truths has God shown me?

Faith Reaches Beyond

from *On the Highroad of Surrender*

Whatever things you ask when you pray, believe
that you receive them, and you will have them.

MARK 11:24 NKJV

Faith, My child, reaches out beyond the need and into the supply.
Always remember that the supply is
greater than the need.

Do you need forgiveness? Lo, I
have provided enough that if all human souls ever created turned to Me
in repentance, they would be fully
pardoned. Will I then deem your sins
too great for remission?

Do you need power to overcome
temptation? Lo, I have overcome, and
in Me there is victory for every soul
that casts itself upon My mercy.

It is patience for which you pray?
Know that in the Spirit there is no
time, and that for which you wait is
already given and only waits your
receiving.

Do I trust God to supply all my needs?

The Divine Commission

from *Come Away My Beloved*

And He said unto them, "Go into all the world,
and preach the gospel to every creature."

MARK 16:15 NJKV

M y child, do not chafe at the bit. It is I who have put it in your mouth. You question My direction because it is not the common way. But I would have you take a path that is quite different from the paths of your friends, and it is because I would bring you into a place in Me and a ministry in which they have no part.

Do not hesitate, and do not falter. In this hour you should be gripped with one consuming purpose—to find the place I have for you.

Your heart will grow cold unless you keep it close to Mine. Your love shall be turned to indifference unless you keep the cross before your eyes.

Have I found God's place for me?

May 29

Exercise Your Faith

from Progress of Another Pilgrim

And they went forth, and preached every where, the
Lord working with them, and confirming the word
with signs following. Amen.

<small>MARK 16:20</small>

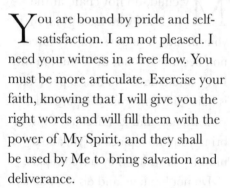

Y̶ou are bound by pride and self-
satisfaction. I am not pleased. I
need your witness in a free flow. You
must be more articulate. Exercise your
faith, knowing that I will give you the
right words and will fill them with the
power of My Spirit, and they shall
be used by Me to bring salvation and
deliverance.

Be not detained by self-doubt. Rely
on Me, and do not regard your own
limitations as a liability.

I will manifest through you in a
mighty way if you will only give Me
the opportunity. Be My mouthpiece,
and I will supply the words and the
message.

*Am I relying on God or focused on my
limitations?*

A Door of Utterance

from *Progress of Another Pilgrim*

And they went forth, and preached every where, the Lord working with them, and confirming the word with signs following. Amen.

MARK 16:20

Behold, I set before you a door of utterance. You shall open your mouth, and I will fill it. You shall go and not be detained. You shall glorify Me, and your own vessel shall be an open channel for the river of My grace.

You shall bring healing. You shall bring hope. I shall endue you with power from on high, and I shall magnify My word so that as you speak it forth I will confirm it, even with miracles following. Be faithful, and deliver My word, and I will surely bless it and cause it to be a creative word, a life-giving word, yes, a word of deliverance.

What words has God put into my mouth?

Call of the Turtledove

from Come Away My Beloved

When Elizabeth heard the greeting of Mary. . .
the babe leaped in her womb; and Elizabeth was
filled with the Holy Spirit.

LUKE 1:41 NKJV

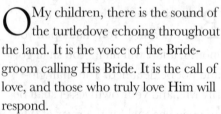

O My children, there is the sound of the turtledove echoing throughout the land. It is the voice of the Bridegroom calling His Bride. It is the call of love, and those who truly love Him will respond.

Like attracts like; and love has always been the test of true discipleship. Those listening to the voice of their Beloved will not be deafened by the cries of men. In a world filled with noises, they will hear Him.

Yes, they shall even hear the tender cooing of the turtledove! Like Elizabeth when she was greeted by Mary, the response was an inner, involuntary response to the nearness of the Christ.

Anticipate Me. Watch for Me. Your heart will listen, and your heart shall hear.

What has my heart heard from God?

Love Endures

from *On the Highroad of Surrender*

He has filled the hungry with good things,
And the rich He has sent away empty.

LUKE 1:53 NKJV

Through many bewildering experiences I deal with the soul. When there is submission of spirit, all things work together for good.

The soul that submits to My disciplines loves Me. Love will hold you steady beneath the chastening rod because love believes and hopes in all things (1 Corinthians 13:7). Love will never fail. It will endure whatever comes because it rests in Me rather than in the circumstance.

You need never be deprived of comfort as long as your desires are fulfilled in Me; for I satisfy the hungry with good things, while the rich go empty away (Luke 1:53). He who goes away will always be empty in spite of his riches. He who seeks Me will never be unhappy or poor.

Is my spirit submitted to Him?

June 2

I Control the Winds

from *Come Away My Beloved*

Guide our feet into the way of peace.
LUKE 1:79

My child, do not be dismayed by any calamity that befalls you. Your times are in My hand. Never doubt My care. Never question My dealings. I am leading you by the narrowness of the way. It is often a difficult and precipitous path; but I would assure you of My hand of protection.

Put your life in My hands, and it will be for you a place of peace and of spiritual comfort. So long as you abide in this place, I will control the rains that fall upon you and the winds that blow. So long as you are in My hands, you are in a garrison the walls of which no enemy will scale.

Have I put my life fully in His hands?

Be Deaf to the Cry of the Crowd

from *On the Highroad of Surrender*

Then passing through the midst of them,
He went His way.

LUKE 4:30 NKJV

A h, My child, this is the secret! Always there will be those who are crowding the way. They will seem to cover the path. If you give power to their words and actions, they will encompass you and prevent your moving ahead. Go your way.

The moment you set your spiritual eye upon the goal I have given you, the bondage of people is broken. You will be able, as Jesus was, to pass through the midst of them and be freed to be about your Father's business. Do not allow yourself to be trapped by the multitude. Your own higher vision will free you, and there is a path in the Spirit, if you walk in it, where there is free motion.

How much have I let the crowd affect my spiritual walk?

The Gift of Forgiveness

from *Come Away My Beloved*

Launch out into the deep and
let down your nets for a catch.
LUKE 5:4 NJKV

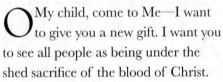

O My child, come to Me—I want to give you a new gift. I want you to see all people as being under the shed sacrifice of the blood of Christ.

He has died for all. His forgiveness encompasses all. Tell them the Good News. It is the confidence in your own heart that will engender faith to receive within the hearts of others.

Freely forgive all, as you have freely loved all. Those to whom you extend My forgiveness will come to experience it for themselves. It is like extending a helping hand to lift another across a brook. Having gained the safety of the other side, he needs your help no longer but stands as secure as yourself; but he needed assistance in crossing over.

Who can I share Jesus with today?

Mercy

from On the Highroad of Surrender

But love your enemies, do good, and lend, hoping
for nothing in return; and your reward will be
great, and you will be sons of the Most High. For
He is kind to the unthankful and evil. Therefore be
merciful, just as your Father also is merciful.

LUKE 6:35–36 NKJV

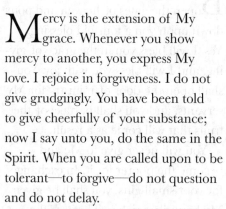

Mercy is the extension of My
grace. Whenever you show
mercy to another, you express My
love. I rejoice in forgiveness. I do not
give grudgingly. You have been told
to give cheerfully of your substance;
now I say unto you, do the same in the
Spirit. When you are called upon to be
tolerant—to forgive—do not question
and do not delay.

Deal justly, but in patience and
understanding, and add not evil
upon evil. As I have given to you, so
likewise do you to others, otherwise
you violate My mercy as it would flow
through you.

Who should I show mercy to today?

The Economy of the Kingdom

from *Come Away My Beloved*

For with the same measure that you use, it will be
measured back to you.

LUKE 6:38 NKJV

———————

Bring Me all the tithes, and I will open the gates of heaven and pour down upon you a fourfold blessing. Yes, I will bless you in the grace of giving, and I will bless you with joy. You shall open the door of ministry for My servants, and you shall partake of the fruits that will come as a result.

You will never give to Me and become the poorer for it. In exchange for your small gifts, you shall be given My boundless riches. Through the contribution that comes from a willing heart, I will be freed to bestow the abundance of heaven, treasures you could never purchase from the world.

With what measure am I giving?

Humbled Hearts

from *Come Away My Beloved*

How can you say. . . "Brother, let me remove the
speck that is in your eye," when you yourself do
not see the plank that is in your own eye?
LUKE 6:42 NKJV

O My people, I have called you to
repentance and confession and
forgiveness and cleansing; but you
have listened to My words as though
they were of little consequence.
Behold, I say: You cannot resist My
Spirit without suffering pain; and you
cannot turn a deaf ear to My words
without falling into the snare of the
enemy.

Look no more to My hand to supply freely your needs when you have
not cleansed your hands and come to
Me with a broken and a contrite heart.
You need not expect Me to speak to
you when your ears are heavy from
listening to evil reports.

How humble is my heart?

On Doing the Father's Work

from *Come Away My Beloved*

Every tree is known by its own fruit. For men do
not gather figs from thorns, nor do they gather
grapes from a bramble bush.

LUKE 6:44 NKJV

Behold, there is a day coming
when you will regret your lethargy,
and you will ask, "Why did we leave
the vineyard of the Lord untended?"
Those things that have occupied you will
appear for what they are—chaff and
worthlessness. For there will be nothing
of lasting value, and no reward for the
works of your hands which you have
done in your own strength, and which I
have not commanded you to do.

I have fashioned you for better things.
Do not fail Me. Place your life under My
divine control and learn to live in the full
blessing of My highest will.

I will strengthen you and comfort
you; I will lead you by the hand.

Is my life under God's control?

Seers

from *On the Highroad of Surrender*

Therefore take heed how you hear. For whoever
has, to him more will be given; and whoever does
not have, even what he seems to have will be
taken from him.

LUKE 8:18 NKJV

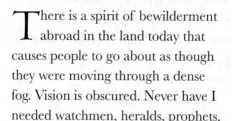

There is a spirit of bewilderment abroad in the land today that causes people to go about as though they were moving through a dense fog. Vision is obscured. Never have I needed watchmen, heralds, prophets, and seers as I need them in this hour.

Stay close to Me no matter what attractions exert themselves to draw you away. I need more time with you, and you need to give fuller attention to the things of the Spirit.

You can never fail to hear My voice if your ears have been un-stopped by obedience and the desire to please and serve Me.

What do I need to do to hear God's voice?

A Fresh Move of Faith

from *On the Highroad of Surrender*

No one, having put his hand to the plow, and
looking back, is fit for the kingdom of God.

LUKE 9:62 NKJV

Believe Me for new things. Venture
forth in trust. It is time to thrust
forward in a new spearhead, a fresh
move of faith. Fight procrastination as
you would resist evil, for surely it is the
enemy of good.

Put forth your hand to the plow
and look not back, neither count the
cost. I will repay you in the currency
of eternity. Keep your eyes on Me and
walk humbly. You are not to doctor
the souls of others, but introduce them
to the Great Physician and provide
a spiritually healthy atmosphere for
those who seek help.

In what ways do I procrastinate?

Disappointment

from On the Highroad of Surrender

No one, having put his hand to the plow, and
looking back, is fit for the kingdom of God.

LUKE 9:62 NKJV

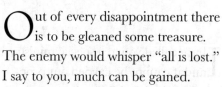

Out of every disappointment there
is to be gleaned some treasure.
The enemy would whisper "all is lost."
I say to you, much can be gained.

Refuse the temptation to brood
over what is gone. It has passed into
the area of My sovereignty. The present challenge requires your undivided
attention.

Give no time to dark thoughts.
Depression undermines the vigor of
the soul.

How do I respond to disappointment?

June 12

An Anointed Tongue

from *Progress of Another Pilgrim*

After these things the Lord appointed other
seventy also, and sent them two and two before his
face into every city and place, whither he
himself would come.

LUKE 10:1

———— ✥ ————

I have called you to a special ministry,
and it cannot be carried out properly without My full blessing.

Let Me anoint your tongue, and
you shall speak with divine authority
and never again will you say, "I am a
weak and inadequate vessel." I shall
put words into your heart and speak
them forth from your lips, and hearts
shall burn as the message goes out.

You shall know that it is My message and My words that are spoken.
The fruits you shall offer up to Me, for
you shall know truly that it is the Lord
your God who has brought to pass His
own word of promise.

What kind of speech comes off my tongue?

Speak the Word of Faith

from *On the Highroad of Surrender*

The harvest truly is great, but the laborers are few;
therefore pray the Lord of the harvest to send out
laborers into His harvest.

LUKE 10:2 NKJV

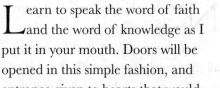

Learn to speak the word of faith and the word of knowledge as I put it in your mouth. Doors will be opened in this simple fashion, and entrance given to hearts that would otherwise have remained closed to the gospel. Once the door is open, you may plant the seed of faith and it will spring forth into eternal life.

Go not to those who are dull of hearing, for their deafness will only increase. Go to the tender, the needy, the brokenhearted, and the suffering. I shall minister in love and compassion, and I shall use you as My mouthpiece.

Do I speak as God commands?

Closed Doors

from *On the Highroad of Surrender*

Behold, I give you the authority to trample on
serpents and scorpions, and over all the power of
the enemy, and nothing shall by any means hurt you.

LUKE 10:19 NKJV

───────────── ❧ ─────────────

Never lose heart when confronted
by disappointment.

Remember always that I control
all that touches you, and as I move
to order your life, I not only open the
right doors, but close the wrong ones.
Whenever a wrong door is closed, it is
by My hand as much as when a right
one opens. In this way I not only bring
you joy but spare you pain. Trust Me.

Have I not said that nothing shall
harm you?

What doors has God opened and closed
in my life?

The Soul Is Directional

from *Progress of Another Pilgrim*

And Jesus answered and said unto her, Martha,
Martha, thou art careful and troubled about many
things: But one thing is needful: and Mary hath
chosen that good part, which shall not be taken
away from her.

LUKE 10:41–42

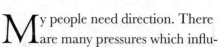

My people need direction. There are many pressures which influence them, but they need to hear a clear voice giving them the wisdom of God.

The soul is directional, and any heart turned toward Me in an attitude of true worship shall receive from Me a quickening flow of life. It cannot be otherwise.

Those who do not hear Me are occupying themselves with other thoughts. They may even be studying the Bible and fail to hear My voice, but they cannot worship Me and miss Me.

What direction is my soul headed in?

Inattention

from *On the Highroad of Surrender*

Therefore take heed that the light which is in you
is not darkness. If then your whole body is full of
light, having no part dark, the whole body will be
full of light, as when the bright shining
of a lamp gives you light.

LUKE 11:35–36 NKJV

If you will listen to My voice, I
will reveal Myself. I am gracious
and patient, but I am grieved by your
hardness of heart and inattention.
Open rebellion usually brings immedi-
ate punishment. Inattention can be even
more destructive to the soul, because it
often goes unnoticed and unrepented,
and is a secret, unexposed sin.

Cast it out in Jesus' Name, and
refuse the robber who would take your
dearest treasure. . .your singleness of
heart in your love for Me.

How single-hearted am I?

No Fear

from *Come Away My Beloved*

Do not fear, little flock, for it is your Father's good
pleasure to give you the kingdom.

LUKE 12:32 NKJV

No, My children, do not fear. Remember the words of Holy Scripture: "Do not fear, little flock, for it is your Father's good pleasure to give you the kingdom" (Luke 12:32). Here you have it again—I am not simply preserving you, but I am doing so for the purpose of sharing with you My kingdom power. If you can catch the vision of what the days ahead hold in store for you in My great kingdom, you will gain a whole new perspective, so that as you view the present, transient scene, its true dimension will come into focus in proportion to the whole panoramic picture.

Am I getting God's picture of my life?

The Highroad of Absolute Surrender

from *On the Highroad of Surrender*

Do not fear, little flock, for it is your Father's good
pleasure to give you the kingdom.

LUKE 12:32 NKJV

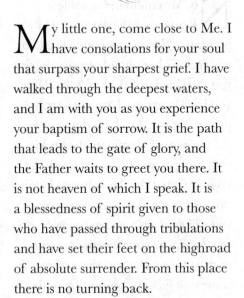

My little one, come close to Me. I have consolations for your soul that surpass your sharpest grief. I have walked through the deepest waters, and I am with you as you experience your baptism of sorrow. It is the path that leads to the gate of glory, and the Father waits to greet you there. It is not heaven of which I speak. It is a blessedness of spirit given to those who have passed through tribulations and have set their feet on the highroad of absolute surrender. From this place there is no turning back.

It may cost you all, but you cannot fathom what I have in store for you.

Hold fast to My hand.

Have I absolutely surrendered to God?

The Sense of Perspective

from Come Away My Beloved

Do not fear, little flock, for it is your Father's good
pleasure to give you the kingdom.

LUKE 12:32 NKJV

———————⟨≫⟩———————

By design of man, out of the
cruelty of wicked hearts, Christ
was made a martyr. But by the Hand
of a greater power, He was made to
become a Savior—even the Savior of
the very men who put Him to death.

My children, do not fear. I am not
simply preserving you, but I am doing
so for the purpose of sharing with you
My kingdom power. If you can catch
the vision of My great kingdom, you
will gain a whole new perspective, so
that as you view the present, transient
scene, its true dimension will come
into focus in proportion to the whole
panoramic picture.

Look at your own life from My
vantage point.

*How can I see my life from
God's vantage point?*

Be Much with Me

from Come Away My Beloved

Therefore you also be ready, for the Son of Man is
coming at an hour you do not expect.

LUKE 12:40 NKJV

———— ❧ ————

My people, set the watch in the
nighttime; yes, rise and pray,
and do not let that hour come upon
you unaware.

For the time is short; yes, the storm
is gathering fast. Can you not discern
the events that are currently shaping up in the affairs of men, and be
as keen to observe their portent and
know that disaster and holocaust are
in the making?

Be more with Me, and let My Spirit
pervade your spirit, and you shall be
more influenced by Me than by the
world around you.

Be much with Me, for there is a
great and heavy burden on My heart.

How can I be often with Him?

I Shall Come Singing

from Come Away My Beloved

Be ready, for the Son of Man is coming
at an hour you do not expect.
LUKE 12:40 NKJV

―――――――――❧―――――――――

My children, be silent before Me. I will lift up My voice as the sound of a trumpet—I will speak clearly to you, for the hour is at hand.

Be obedient, and raise your standards of discipline and dedication to a higher level. For My face is set toward My imminent return to earth. I wait only the release from the Father's hand.

Though I am ready and longing to come to you, you are not yet ready. You have spurned My entreaties, and you have fought against the restraints of the Spirit.

Keep your vision filled with Me. Keep your life in tune and your worship in mutual harmony.

For I will come singing, and what will you be if you are in discord?

Is my life in tune with God's will?

Harmony of Purpose

from *Progress of Another Pilgrim*

Whosoever. . .forsaketh not all that he hath,
he cannot be my disciple.
LUKE 14:33

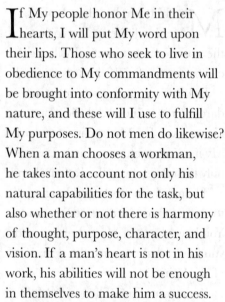

If My people honor Me in their
hearts, I will put My word upon
their lips. Those who seek to live in
obedience to My commandments will
be brought into conformity with My
nature, and these will I use to fulfill
My purposes. Do not men do likewise?
When a man chooses a workman,
he takes into account not only his
natural capabilities for the task, but
also whether or not there is harmony
of thought, purpose, character, and
vision. If a man's heart is not in his
work, his abilities will not be enough
in themselves to make him a success.

Many are zealous and eager to
serve in the Kingdom, but I cannot
use them because their desires and
goals are at cross-purposes with Mine.

What are my real desires and goals?

Simplicity of Spirit

from *Progress of Another Pilgrim*

Whosoever shall not receive the kingdom of God
as a little child shall in no wise enter therein.

LUKE 18:17

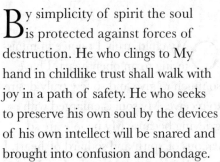

By simplicity of spirit the soul is protected against forces of destruction. He who clings to My hand in childlike trust shall walk with joy in a path of safety. He who seeks to preserve his own soul by the devices of his own intellect will be snared and brought into confusion and bondage.

The soul progresses by praise, worship, and love, but it is hindered by conscious thought and effort. Jesus taught this in His reference to the lilies of the field, how they neither toil nor spin, but are clothed by the Father.

Lay at My feet the anxiety about your own spiritual life, and give yourself to love Me and to worship Me. The results in your soul will be joy and victory.

Is my spirit simple or anxious?

I Await Your Desire

from *Progress of Another Pilgrim*

Now when Jesus heard these things, he said unto him, Yet lackest thou one thing: sell all that thou hast, and distribute unto the poor, and thou shalt have treasure in heaven: and come, follow me.

Luke 18:22

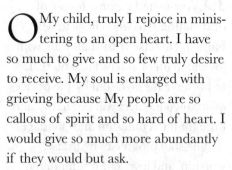

O My child, truly I rejoice in ministering to an open heart. I have so much to give and so few truly desire to receive. My soul is enlarged with grieving because My people are so callous of spirit and so hard of heart. I would give so much more abundantly if they would but ask.

I await your desire, because if I gave to you when your desire was small, you would not be prepared for receiving.

Hide nothing from Me. Bring Me everything, and repent of anything you cannot offer Me as a holy gift. I would sanctify your entire life. Release all to Me.

Have I released all to Him?

A Crucial Hour

from *Progress of Another Pilgrim*

Watch ye therefore, and pray always, that ye may
be accounted worthy to escape all these things that
shall come to pass, and to stand before the
Son of man.

LUKE 21:36

Watch for the signs of My soon-coming. Do not be blind to
that which is transpiring around you
and in the world. It has been revealed
to you what you may expect. No
concern lies more heavily on My heart
than the preparation of My chosen
ones for the ingathering. I do not want
My coming to be so and catch you
by surprise. Not only do you need to
prepare your own hearts, but I would
use you to warn and help others.

This is no time for apathy. There
has been no more crucial hour in all
man's history.

*How prepared is my heart for the
Lord's coming?*

Anticipation, Meditation, Participation

from *On the Highroad of Surrender*

And in the daytime He was teaching in the temple,
but at night He went out and stayed on the mountain
called Olivet. Then early in the morning all the
people came to Him in the temple
to hear Him.

Luke 21:37–38 NKJV

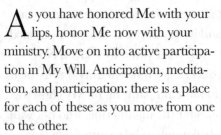

As you have honored Me with your lips, honor Me now with your ministry. Move on into active participation in My Will. Anticipation, meditation, and participation: there is a place for each of these as you move from one to the other.

Never get bogged down at any one of these points. Solitude and then service, and vice-versa. Neither is complete in itself. Each is enriched by the other. In solitude I minister to you, and in service I minister through you to others. Both are essential to your growth, and others are robbed of blessing if you hoard the riches of God and fail to share.

How much time do I make for solitude before God?

The Rod and the Look

from On the Highroad of Surrender

Then Peter remembered the word of the Lord,
how He had said to him, "Before the rooster
crows, you will deny Me three times." So Peter
went out and wept bitterly.

LUKE 22:61–62 NKJV

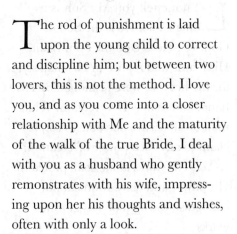

The rod of punishment is laid upon the young child to correct and discipline him; but between two lovers, this is not the method. I love you, and as you come into a closer relationship with Me and the maturity of the walk of the true Bride, I deal with you as a husband who gently remonstrates with his wife, impressing upon her his thoughts and wishes, often with only a look.

Just to draw near Me in a time of failure brings to the sensitive, loving spirit deeper suffering than was ever brought to a disobedient child by the chastening rod.

Does God use a rod or a look with me?

June 28

Exalt His Name

from Progress of Another Pilgrim

In the beginning was the Word, and the Word was
with God, and the Word was God. The same was
in the beginning with God.

JOHN 1:1–2

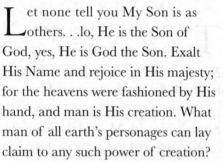

Let none tell you My Son is as
others. . .lo, He is the Son of
God, yes, He is God the Son. Exalt
His Name and rejoice in His majesty;
for the heavens were fashioned by His
hand, and man is His creation. What
man of all earth's personages can lay
claim to any such power of creation?

Yes, His works alone shall proclaim
His power and deity. Man cannot
extinguish the light of His glorious
works.

*What do I say when others deny
Jesus is God?*

The Cross in the Star

from *On the Highroad of Surrender*

The Word became flesh and dwelt among us,
and we beheld His glory, the glory as of the only
begotten of the Father, full of grace and truth.

JOHN 1:14 NKJV

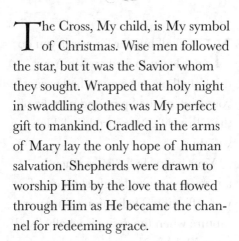

The Cross, My child, is My symbol of Christmas. Wise men followed the star, but it was the Savior whom they sought. Wrapped that holy night in swaddling clothes was My perfect gift to mankind. Cradled in the arms of Mary lay the only hope of human salvation. Shepherds were drawn to worship Him by the love that flowed through Him as He became the channel for redeeming grace.

*How have I praised God for His
salvation through Jesus?*

The Central Object

from Progress of Another Pilgrim

> But whosoever drinketh of the water that I shall
> give him shall never thirst; but the water that I shall
> give him shall be in him a well of water springing
> up into everlasting life.
>
> JOHN 4:14

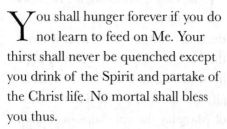

Y ou shall hunger forever if you do
not learn to feed on Me. Your
thirst shall never be quenched except
you drink of the Spirit and partake of
the Christ life. No mortal shall bless
you thus.

Your heart shall rejoice when I
am the central and highest object of
your affection. Dedication brings pure
rapture when the desire is wholly fixed
upon Me! My Name alone, when
breathed in adoration, lifts the weari-
est heart from despair and fills the
seeking soul with exhilaration.

*Is Jesus the central object of affection in
my life?*

You Shall Not Be Earthbound

from *Come Away My Beloved*

Whoever drinks of the water that I shall give him will never thirst. But the water that I shall give him will become in him a fountain of water springing up into everlasting life.

JOHN 4:14 NKJV

O My children, what do you need today? I assure you, whatever you need, if you will look to Me, I will supply.

I will give you life, light, and strength. I will surround you and preserve you, so that in Me you may live, move, and have your being, existing in Me when apart from Me you would die.

You will live in a realm where the things of earth will not be able to limit your movement; but you will be freed in Me to a place where your spirit may soar as the eagle.

Does my spirit soar like an eagle?

Keep Your Channel Clear

from *Come Away My Beloved*

Whoever drinks of the water that I shall give him
will never thirst. But the water that I shall give him
will become in him a fountain of water springing
up into everlasting life.

JOHN 4:14 NKJV

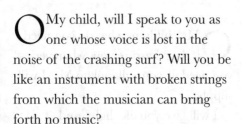

O My child, will I speak to you as
one whose voice is lost in the
noise of the crashing surf? Will you be
like an instrument with broken strings
from which the musician can bring
forth no music?

No, I would have you be as the wa-
terfall whose sound is continuous, as a
great river whose flow is not interrupt-
ed. You shall not sing for a time and
then be silent for a season. You shall
not praise for a day and then revert to
the current topics of everyday life.

Is my voice continuous in praise?

The Healing Pool

from *Progress of Another Pilgrim*

For an angel went down at a certain season into the pool, and troubled the water: whosoever then first after the troubling of the water stepped in was made whole of whatsoever disease he had.

JOHN 5:4

Whenever you are in any kind of trouble, know that My Spirit in the midst is like the angel who stirred the Pool of Bethesda and made it a place of healing. Disturbances which give every appearance of being natural become infused with divine purposes if your soul is allowed to lie in My hand.

You need not discern every experience in order to receive a blessing. I Myself touch circumstances and add the power of the miraculous, and you shall many times be startled to discover the reflection of My face in a very ordinary "pool."

Where have I seen the reflection of His face?

Mighty Triumph

from *Dialogues with God*

*He that heareth my word, and believeth on him
that sent me, hath everlasting life, and shall not
come into condemnation; but is passed
from death unto life.*

JOHN 5:24

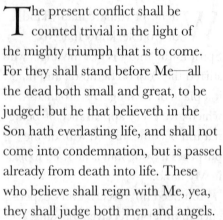

The present conflict shall be counted trivial in the light of the mighty triumph that is to come. For they shall stand before Me—all the dead both small and great, to be judged: but he that believeth in the Son hath everlasting life, and shall not come into condemnation, but is passed already from death into life. These who believe shall reign with Me, yea, they shall judge both men and angels.

Hearken to My words in John 15 and simply abide in Me as the branch in the vine. Make this present moment one of victory in Me, and live moment by moment, lost in My love.

*How confident am I in God's
mighty triumph?*

The Apple of My Eye

from *Come Away My Beloved*

He who hears My word and believes in Him who
sent Me has everlasting life, and shall not come
into judgment, but has passed from death into life.
JOHN 5:24 NKJV

O My little ones, you are the apple of My eye, I will guard you from harm. Never let the fears that are common to the world creep into your hearts, for you are not of the world, and you need not fear the things that plague the minds of the ungodly.

You need not fear the coming judgment, for if your sins have been confessed and forgiven and cleansed by the blood of Jesus, you will not be condemned, because you are already passed from death into eternal life. You need not fear the Day of Judgment. It is sent to try the world, and you are not of the world, My little children.

What do I fear?

Only by a Person

from *Progress of Another Pilgrim*

I am the living bread which came down from
heaven: if any man eat of this bread, he shall live
for ever: and the bread that I will give is my flesh,
which I will give for the life of the world.

JOHN 6:51

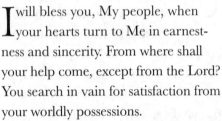

I will bless you, My people, when
your hearts turn to Me in earnest-
ness and sincerity. From where shall
your help come, except from the Lord?
You search in vain for satisfaction from
your worldly possessions.

Your soul can be nourished only
by a person—not by any thing; and
the only person adequate to meet the
hunger of your soul is the Person of
the Lord Jesus Christ, through the
ministry of the blessed Holy Spirit.

Where is my heart turned?

Safety in God's Will

from *Come Away My Beloved*

If anyone is a worshiper of God and does His will,
He hears him.

JOHN 9:31 NKJV

M y will is not a place, but a condition. Do not ask Me where and when, but ask Me how. You will discover blessing in every place, and any place, if your spirit is in tune with Me.

I direct every motion of your life, as the ocean bears a ship. Your will and intelligence may be at the helm, but divine providence and sovereignty are stronger forces. You can trust Me, knowing that any pressure I bring to bear upon your life is initiated by My love.

Move on steadily, and know that the waters that carry you are the waters of My love and My kindness, and I will keep you on the right course.

What course is my life on?

July 8

Stay Pliable in My Hand

from *Come Away My Beloved*

I have come that they may have life, and that they
may have it more abundantly.
JOHN 10:10 NKJV

O My child, be quick to obey. For the
moving of My Spirit may at times
be inconvenient to the flesh, and may at
other times be diametrically opposed to
reason, but obey Me regardless of the
cost. You will always be amply repaid
for any sacrifice with an abundance of
blessing.

I will not force you to make the
choice, nor make My will inescapable.
There will always be an easier way open
to you, one that will seem more reasonable, involving less risk. I have calculated
the risk to test and develop your faith
as well as your obedience, and in the
choosing process, I give you an opportunity to prove your love for Me.

Be sensitive to My Spirit.

How sensitive am I to the Spirit?

Put Off the Self-Life

from *Progress of Another Pilgrim*

If ye know these things, happy are ye if
ye do them.
JOHN 13:17

Be aware of My presence. Your receptivity is dulled by undue involvement in unimportant pastimes. I need your full attention, yes, I need complete dedication.

These are the closing hours of this dispensation, and I am calling all My chosen to put off the self-life and to walk in the Spirit. This is not a new message. It was the message of the apostles; indeed, it was the message of Jesus. It was also the message of the Psalms and Proverbs, insofar as they emphasize uncompromising loyalty to the truth, and outward actions that are consistent with inward convictions.

How might my self-life be stunting my spiritual growth?

The Spirit of Life

from *Dialogues with God*

Greater works than I do shall ye do,
because I go unto my Father.

JOHN 14:12

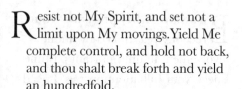

Resist not My Spirit, and set not a limit upon My movings. Yield Me complete control, and hold not back, and thou shalt break forth and yield an hundredfold.

My Spirit is the Spirit of Life, and I am in thee and upon thee that thou shouldst not be barren nor unfruitful;

and whomsoever thou touchest in faith shall feel My quickening power. Life shall rise out of death; yea, Eternal Life out of spiritual death.

Is this not even greater than My servant Lazarus?

For I said, "Greater works than I do shall ye do, because I go unto my Father" (John 14:12).

The world seeth me not—but ye see me, and because I live, ye shall live also.

How do I resist the Spirit?

Rewards of Devotion

from *On the Highroad of Surrender*

He who has My commandments and keeps them,
it is he who loves Me. And he who loves Me will
be loved by My Father, and I will love him and
manifest Myself to him.

JOHN 14:21 NKJV

A s your soul turns to worship, let
it be with one supreme desire: to
bring Me your love. Eternity will be a
time of rejoicing because all will love
Me and find expression for their love.
This is not a selfish demand on My
part. I can ask of you a full portion,
yes, unlimited devotion, because I am
a giver, not a taker, and you will always
find yourself enriched beyond your ex-
pectations whenever you give yourself
to me in even a very limited way.

I ask you to give only to bless you
more.

*When have I experienced God's blessing
through obedience?*

July 12

Renew Your Vows

from Come Away My Beloved

He who has My commandments and keeps them,
it is he who loves Me. And he who loves Me will
be loved by My Father, and I will love him and
manifest Myself to him.

JOHN 14:21 NKJV

There is a day coming when you
will say, "I have waited in vain
for the Lord." You will wait for Me
to speak, and you will hear only the
whistling of the wind. But I tell you
now, I am never silent; you are deaf. I
am always speaking; but I do not find
your ear attuned to listen.

You will sit alone in a desolate place
and grieve in your loneliness; but it
will not be that I have left you, but that
you have become insensitive to My
presence.

Confess your coldness, and draw
near to Me. Renew your vows, and I
will revive your ministry.

*How have I been insensitive to God's
presence?*

Strivings Hinder

from *Progress of Another Pilgrim*

Jesus answered and said unto him, If a man love me, he will keep my words: and my Father will love him, and we will come unto him, and make our abode with him.

JOHN 14:23

My people are drifting like a boat with empty sails. But I shall blow, saith the Lord; yes, I shall cause a mighty wind to rise, and the sails shall be filled, and the Spirit shall drive you forward. You shall rejoice in Me and praise My Name.

In your own power you can accomplish nothing whatsoever in the kingdom of God. I need your submission, but I do not need your help.

All strivings only hinder. Love is the only telling contribution you can make toward the perfecting of your soul.

Am I striving or submitting?

The Glory of My Presence

from *Dialogues with God*

My peace I give unto you; not as the world giveth,
give I unto you. Let not your heart be troubled,
neither let it be afraid.

JOHN 14:27

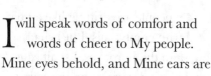

I will speak words of comfort and
words of cheer to My people.
Mine eyes behold, and Mine ears are
open, and lo, All through the
night have I stood watch.
Through the darkness have I set limits
for thy protection, and lo, the
enemy cannot break through the
lines. For I have set a limit to his
power, and I have curtailed his
activities.
I am in the midst of My people to give
them peace. I shall dine with them
at the table, though countless
hosts encamp round about.
I shall cover them with My almighty
hand.

How much of God's peace am I enjoying?

The Shadow of My Hand

from *On the Highroad of Surrender*

Peace I leave with you, My peace I give to you; not as the world gives do I give to you. Let not your heart be troubled, neither let it be afraid.

JOHN 14:27 NKJV

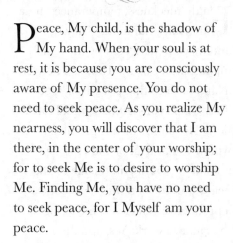

Peace, My child, is the shadow of My hand. When your soul is at rest, it is because you are consciously aware of My presence. You do not need to seek peace. As you realize My nearness, you will discover that I am there, in the center of your worship; for to seek Me is to desire to worship Me. Finding Me, you have no need to seek peace, for I Myself am your peace.

Is my soul at rest?

The Father's Husbandry

from Progress of Another Pilgrim

I am the true vine, and my Father is the husbandman.

JOHN 15:1

Faith, meekness, temperance: these are fruits that mature slowly, and they are perfected by the careful husbandry of the Father. There is a kind of faith that is a gift of God. This is believing faith for initial salvation. The faith which is produced within you as fruit of the Holy Spirit is a faith operating in the life of the believer to the end that he becomes a productive vehicle for the doing of the Father's work. Yes, and this fruit of meekness goes beyond mildness of temperament, even to an acceptance of injustice. It is not only patient, but gracious—returning good for evil. This is verily a divine fruit. This you may experience as you yield fully to My Spirit within.

What kind of fruit am I bearing?

Fulfillment

from *Progress of Another Pilgrim*

Herein is my Father glorified, that ye bear much
fruit; so shall ye be my disciples.

JOHN 15:8

E very door that I open, you shall
pass through. My Spirit shall
speak, and you shall utter that which is
given unto you.

You have been like a green plant.
Now I would have you put forth blossoms. The flowering is a symbol of the
manifestation of the Spirit. Yes, it is
even more; it is fulfillment of original
purpose. It is destiny. It is the ultimate
end to which it was designated by the
Creator. Anything less would be failure
and disappointment.

Only to have life is not enough. Fulfillment is that for which I am waiting,
yes, the manifestation of My sons and
daughters as they come to maturity
and as they produce that for which I
created them.

How am I fulfilling God's purpose in my life?

Pretense Will Not Worship

from *On the Highroad of Surrender*

When He, the Spirit of truth, has come,
He will guide you into all truth.
JOHN 16:13 NKJV

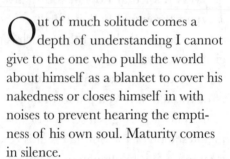

Out of much solitude comes a depth of understanding I cannot give to the one who pulls the world about himself as a blanket to cover his nakedness or closes himself in with noises to prevent hearing the emptiness of his own soul. Maturity comes in silence.

Only prayer furnishes the soul with nourishment; but prayer itself must be born of singleness of heart. Pretense will not enter the gate of worship. Pretense will stand outside and flaunt its own self-proclaimed piety. I would have you true and honest. Better to be a sinner and confess it than to profess purity you do not possess.

Search your heart in the light of My Word. Let the Holy Spirit give insight.

How true and honest is my heart?

The Healing Power
of Joy

from *Come Away My Beloved*

You will be sorrowful, but your sorrow
will be turned into joy.

JOHN 16:20 NKJV

Distress of soul and grief of heart can only bring on destruction of body. Joy alone is a healer, and you can have it in the darkest hour if you will force your soul to rise to me in worship and adoration.

Bring Me your sorrow, and watch for the sunrise of the resurrection. Truly there comes a morning when hope is reborn and life finds new beginning. Wait for it as tulip bulbs anticipate the spring. The rarest blooms are enhanced by the coldness of winter. The snow plays her part in producing spring's pageant. But when the blossoms break through, we do not then turn back to thoughts of winter, but instead, we look ahead to the full joys of the coming summer.

What sorrows can I trade for God's joy?

Union of Spirit

from *Progress of Another Pilgrim*

I in them, and thou in me, that they may be made
perfect in one; and that the world may know that
thou hast sent me, and hast loved them,
as thou hast loved me.

JOHN 17:23

T here is a flow of divine life, and as you enter into it, you shall find victory. If you long to see your own personal wishes subjugated to the will and purposes of God, let your heart be at rest. For this union of your spirit with My Spirit and of your will and My will shall come as simply and easily as rain falling, if you can learn this one secret, that is, how to lose yourself in the flow of My life as I live within you.

Am I truly united with God's Spirit?

You Cannot Weary My Love

from *Come Away My Beloved*

Then saith he to Thomas, Reach hither thy finger,
and behold my hands; and reach hither thy hand,
and thrust it into my side: and be not
faithless, but believing.

JOHN 20:27

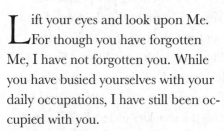

L ift your eyes and look upon Me. For though you have forgotten Me, I have not forgotten you. While you have busied yourselves with your daily occupations, I have still been occupied with you.

My little children, you cannot weary My love. You may grieve My heart, but My love is changeless, infinite. I long for you to turn to Me. My hands are full of blessings that I desire to give you. I long to hear your voice. You speak much with others—O speak to Me! I have so much to tell you.

How often do I speak with God?

Break Loose the Fetters

from Come Away My Beloved

But you shall receive power when the Holy Spirit
has come upon you; and you shall be witnesses to
Me. . .to the end of the earth.

ACTS 1:8 NKJV

With a strong and mighty hand I will bring My people out. Yes, as I brought the children of Israel out from the bondage of Egypt and Pharaoh; with a yet greater form of liberation I will bring My people out from under the yoke of false prophets and the shackles of legalism. Do not be afraid to follow Me. For one of these days the curtain will be drawn; the heavens will be rolled back; the canopy of the sky as you know it will be lifted away; and the Son of Man shall be revealed in power and great glory.

Break loose the fetters. Cast off the fears. Walk forth in the conquering strength of My Holy Spirit.

What fears bind me?

The Dynamic of Miracles

from *Progress of Another Pilgrim*

But ye shall receive power, after that the Holy
Ghost is come upon you: and ye shall be witnesses
unto me both in Jerusalem, and in all Judaea,
and in Samaria, and unto the uttermost
part of the earth.

ACTS 1:8

O My child, lie quietly in My hand.
The dynamic of miracles is here.
Your own weakness is of no consequence, for I would vest you with My
power. Your insignificance shall be
swallowed up in My Presence.

My Presence is all about you, even
all through you. Unless you resist Me,
you cannot fail, for I cannot fail and
you are in Me, kept by the power of
God. Strengthen your heart with this
truth.

How quiet am I in God's hand?

July 24

Give Yourself to Prayer and the Word

from *Progress of Another Pilgrim*

But we will give ourselves continually to prayer,
and to the ministry of the word.

ACTS 6:4

Give yourself to a life of prayer and much careful study of the Word, that you may be able to give My message with clarity and the unction of the Holy Spirit.

Dispose of nonessentials. Concentrate your thoughts and intentions upon Jesus Christ, and in Him seek your wisdom and comfort. I will open avenues to aid you, for this is My will for you, and you can know that I will always make a way for the performance of My will in your life once you have set your goal to be obedient to My commands. Is it not written that I give you the desires of your heart? Give yourself to the desire, and I shall give Myself to the fulfillment.

What do I give myself to?

Expect the Unexpected

from Come Away My Beloved

Then Philip went down to the city of Samaria and
preached Christ to them. And the multitudes with
one accord heeded the things spoken by Philip,
hearing and seeing the miracles which he did.

ACTS 8:5–6 NKJV

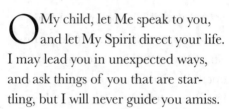

O My child, let Me speak to you,
and let My Spirit direct your life.
I may lead you in unexpected ways,
and ask things of you that are star-
tling, but I will never guide you amiss.

Do not walk according to your natural reasoning, but obey the promptings of the Spirit, and be obedient to
My voice.

You shall go as Philip went—at the
direction of the Spirit—into the places
that are out of the way, and bring light
on My Word to those who are in need.

Stay in an attitude of prayer and
faith, and I will do all the rest.

What is my attitude?

Anticipate Surprises

from *Progress of Another Pilgrim*

And the angel of the Lord spake unto Philip,
saying, Arise, and go toward the south unto the
way that goeth down from Jerusalem unto Gaza,
which is desert.

ACTS 8:26

O My child, be obedient. I have purposes for you. I have a ministry for you. Look not to any man to open this door. I not only open doors, but more often than otherwise, I create the place of service. I make My own plans, and in order to reach the souls for whom I am concerned, I lead in new paths and down unpaved roads.

One Bible example of this is the account of Philip and his witness to the eunuch crossing the desert.

Be prepared for the unexpected, and anticipate surprises if you deign to follow Me.

How prepared am I to serve God in
new ways?

The Ways of the Spirit

from On the Highroad of Surrender

And the men who journeyed with him stood
speechless, hearing a voice but seeing no one.

ACTS 9:7 NKJV

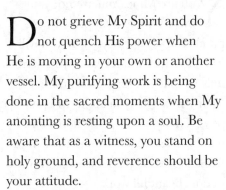

Do not grieve My Spirit and do
not quench His power when
He is moving in your own or another
vessel. My purifying work is being
done in the sacred moments when My
anointing is resting upon a soul. Be
aware that as a witness, you stand on
holy ground, and reverence should be
your attitude.

I reveal to each individual what is
necessary for his own soul's progress.
Others do not need to know. Like Saul
on the road to Damascus, to him were
spoken clear words, while others heard
only a sound. Even so, I speak clearly
to the one who is slain in the Spirit.
Others need not know nor question.

How is my soul's progress?

July 28

A Beautiful Work

from *Come Away My Beloved*

He is a chosen vessel of Mine to bear My name.
ACTS 9:15 NKJV

———————— ❧ ————————

Y ou are Mine. You are not your
own. With a great price I have
purchased you for Myself. If you will
listen to Me, I will reveal to you more
fully so that you may know more
clearly how vital you are to My purpose. There is work to be done, and I
need you as a vessel through which to
work. Not a vassal, but a vessel. I want
to do a beautiful work.

There will be inconveniences to
be borne, self-pleasing to be laid
aside, sacrifices and pain—but what a
blessed reward I have in store! Yes, in
store for you, if you are able to let Me
use you the way I desire.

Lo, I wait for you. Come to Me.

How willing am I to be God's vessel?

Attitude Determines Outcome

from *On the Highroad of Surrender*

I was not disobedient to the heavenly vision.
ACTS 26:19 NKJV

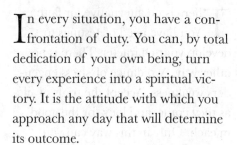

In every situation, you have a confrontation of duty. You can, by total dedication of your own being, turn every experience into a spiritual victory. It is the attitude with which you approach any day that will determine its outcome.

You are not a helpless pawn on a board. You are a child of God with prerogatives for accomplishing His will, not your own. Let this help to bring you guidance when you are in doubt.

Be about your Father's business. There will always be plenty of other people occupied with the affairs of the world.

What spiritual victories am I experiencing?

Hidden Resources

from *Progress of Another Pilgrim*

And not only so, but we glory in tribulations also:
knowing that tribulation worketh patience.

ROMANS 5:3

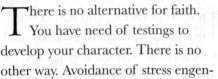

There is no alternative for faith. You have need of testings to develop your character. There is no other way. Avoidance of stress engenders weakness. Accept the trials of life as they come, and look for the good in each. Only in this way can you advance and grow in stature.

Only through much self-discipline and self-denial can you gain the victory.

It is only through the power of My Spirit within you that you shall be able to tap hidden resources that have power to sustain you above yourself. Therefore you are not dependent upon nor limited by the level of your own strength of character, but you may rise above it and lift your own actions up into My divine pattern for you.

What trials are currently helping me to grow?

Kindness

from *On the Highroad of Surrender*

Now hope does not disappoint, because the love of
God has been poured out in our hearts by the Holy
Spirit who was given to us.

ROMANS 5:5 NKJV

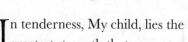

In tenderness, My child, lies the
greatest strength that can come to
the human heart. Kindness is like a
rose, which though easily crushed and
fragile, yet speaks a language of silent
power. It is the same power that lies
in the eyes of one who loves. It is the
power that moves the hands of those
who give alms.

Beauty comes to the inner soul as
tenderness becomes the outer expression. Those who find it have captured
the atmosphere of heaven and have
brought to their human relationships
the essence of God's holy love.

How much tenderness do I offer to those
seeking God's kingdom?

Endurance

from *On the Highroad of Surrender*

Now hope does not disappoint, because the love
of God has been poured out in our hearts by the
Holy Spirit who was given to us.

ROMANS 5:5 NKJV

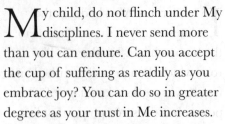

My child, do not flinch under My disciplines. I never send more than you can endure. Can you accept the cup of suffering as readily as you embrace joy? You can do so in greater degrees as your trust in Me increases.

My love never fails, even when it brings you pain. It is in the patient endurance of affliction that the soul is seasoned with grace. It is a barren life that holds only happiness. Saints are not nurtured by levity. Hope does not spring from good fortune.

How have I responded to God's disciplines?

Desire Holiness

from *Make Haste My Beloved*

For sin shall not have dominion over you: for ye
are not under the law, but under grace.
ROMANS 6:14

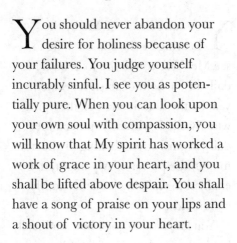

Y ou should never abandon your desire for holiness because of your failures. You judge yourself incurably sinful. I see you as potentially pure. When you can look upon your own soul with compassion, you will know that My spirit has worked a work of grace in your heart, and you shall be lifted above despair. You shall have a song of praise on your lips and a shout of victory in your heart.

Do I desire holiness or give in to despair?

Strengthening Power

from Dialogues with God

For that which I do I allow not: for what I would,
that do I not; but what I hate, that do I.

ROMANS 7:15

You have heard of Me by the hearing of the ear, but long to see Me. Yea, you desire to behold Me daily in the light of fresh revelation, yea, by the illumination of the Spirit who dwelleth within. You need the daily inward strengthening of the new man in the power of My might, to be enabled to walk in obedience to My commands.

You know to do good but continually battle the tendencies of your human nature to do otherwise. For the flesh resisteth the progress of the Spirit (Romans 7:15–25). But as Paul, you make your confession: Thanks be unto God Who giveth us the victory through our Lord Jesus Christ!

Am I daily strengthened by Him?

My Energizing Spirit

from Dialogues with God

But if the Spirit of him that raised up Jesus from the
dead dwell in you, he that raised up Christ from the
dead shall also quicken your mortal bodies by his
Spirit that dwelleth in you.

ROMANS 8:11

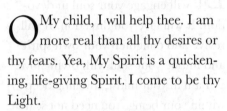

OMy child, I will help thee. I am
more real than all thy desires or
thy fears. Yea, My Spirit is a quickening, life-giving Spirit. I come to be thy
Light.

In My presence there is no darkness. Have ye not read that in the
Eternal City there is no need of can-
dle, nor of the sun or moon, because
the Lamb is the Light of it? Surely if
I can brighten all of Eternity, I have
ample supply to flood thy heart and
mind and thy body with My mighty
power, My light, and My love—My
deep joy and My energizing Spirit.

Ye need not depend upon thine
own limited strength and endurance.

What do I depend on?

Only Yield the Vessel

from *Progress of Another Pilgrim*

For as many as are led by the Spirit of God,
they are the sons of God.

ROMANS 8:14

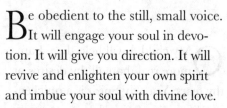

Be obedient to the still, small voice. It will engage your soul in devotion. It will give you direction. It will revive and enlighten your own spirit and imbue your soul with divine love.

I am in your midst, dwelling deep within your being. You need not search for Me any further away than your own heart. I have come to reside there by your own invitation. Do not turn outward again and ignore Me, but look in and know that what I give you to share with others will very truly be not ministering of yourself, but the flowing forth of My Spirit shall move through you and speak through you. Only yield your vessel. He is your victory.

When have I heard God's still, small voice?

Pray and Walk in the Spirit

from *Progress of Another Pilgrim*

For as many as are led by the Spirit of God,
they are the sons of God.

ROMANS 8:14

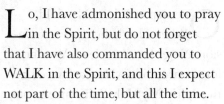

L o, I have admonished you to pray in the Spirit, but do not forget that I have also commanded you to WALK in the Spirit, and this I expect not part of the time, but all the time.

The need is critical, the hour is late, and I am calling for full commitment from My own. You have desired to be chosen. Having been chosen, I would have you understand that I expect far more of you than of those who are not.

How am I praying and walking in His Spirit?

Turbulence, a Warning Signal

from *On the Highroad of Surrender*

For as many as are led by the Spirit of God,
they are sons of God.

ROMANS 8:14

One step at a time, My child. When I lead, there is no confusion. Never let others lead. Your need for confirmation will be answered by the Spirit. My Holy Spirit meets your every need. If it is wisdom that you seek, you will receive it if you draw upon Him. He resides within you to be your all. Never bypass this infinite supply of all goodness. Never move into a new situation until you are at peace about it within your own soul. My Spirit harmonizes all action. If you sense discord or turbulence, know that there is a spiritual battle already on the scene. Let it be a warning signal. Look for the root of it, and do not blindly forge ahead.

Is God's Spirit or another leading me?

The Forces of Intercession

from *Progress of Another Pilgrim*

Likewise the Spirit also helpeth our infirmities: for we know not what we should pray for as we ought: but the Spirit itself maketh intercession for us with groanings which cannot be uttered.

ROMANS 8:26

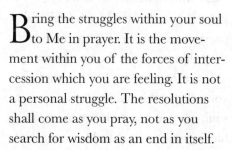

Bring the struggles within your soul to Me in prayer. It is the movement within you of the forces of intercession which you are feeling. It is not a personal struggle. The resolutions shall come as you pray, not as you search for wisdom as an end in itself.

Prayer has brought more illumination than books. Seek Me, and you shall know. You shall understand more than you dream possible, and your inner peace shall deepen.

What struggles should I bring to God?

August 9

The Vineyard of Prayer

from Come Away My Beloved

Now He who searches the hearts knows what the
mind of the Spirit is, because He makes intercession for the saints according to the will of God.

ROMANS 8:27 NKJV

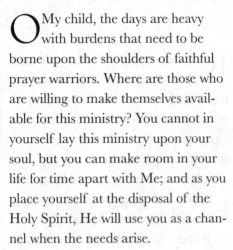

O My child, the days are heavy
with burdens that need to be
borne upon the shoulders of faithful
prayer warriors. Where are those who
are willing to make themselves available for this ministry? You cannot in
yourself lay this ministry upon your
soul, but you can make room in your
life for time apart with Me; and as you
place yourself at the disposal of the
Holy Spirit, He will use you as a channel when the needs arise.

I am calling My Spirit-filled
believers to labor in the vineyard of
prayer. Rejoice to be granted the privilege of so sacred a task. Cherish it and
cultivate it.

How can I cultivate my vineyard of prayer?

Victory in Adversity

from On the Highroad of Surrender

And we know that all things work together for
good to those who love God, to those who are the
called according to His purpose.

ROMANS 8:28 NKJV

Whenever you experience pain,
know that I am knocking at the
door of your heart.

Nothing should be of any real concern to you except your relationship to
Me and a right attitude toward others.
Life brings unpleasant circumstances,
but I say unto you, I am in the midst,
causing all experiences, both pleasant
and otherwise, to harmonize for your
blessing and growth.

I do not shield you from hardship. I
give you victory while in the throes of
adversity.

*How is God working out His victory
in my life?*

Flee Compromise

from *On the Highroad of Surrender*

Nay, in all these things we are more than conquerors
through Him who loved us.

ROMANS 8:37

O My people, the hour is late and the time for sleeping is past. Gird on the armor of truth and righteousness, and know that the battle is in full array.

Not by might nor by power, but by My Spirit shall you be victorious, so do not seek to outwit the enemy by fleshly strategy. Only as you go in the strength of the Lord shall you stand.

Flee compromise, for it leads always to defeat. The shed blood of Christ is your only protection. When you go into battle, go in My Name, and know that you go against an already-defeated foe.

Claim the victory, and know that it is yours as you act in faith, not doubting, not retreating, and not arbitrating with the enemy.

*In what areas am I tempted to
compromise?*

Learn to Reign

from *Come Away My Beloved*

Nay, in all these things we are more than conquerors
through him that loved us.

Romans 8:37

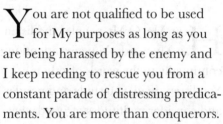

Y ou are not qualified to be used
for My purposes as long as you
are being harassed by the enemy and
I keep needing to rescue you from a
constant parade of distressing predica-
ments. You are more than conquerors.

Rise up, then, and lay claim to the
power that is yours, because I am in
you, and you are in Me, and as I was
in the world, so are you. I was victorious, and you too may be victorious.
I withstood every encounter with the
devil, and you, too, can stand against
him. I healed the sick and wrested
tortured bodies out of the grip of evil
forces, and you, too, can do the same.

Learn to reign, for I have made you
to become kings and priests.

How can I learn to reign?

August 13

The Righteous Remnant

from *On the Highroad of Surrender*

And it shall come to pass in the place where it was
said to them, "You are not My people," There
they shall be called sons of the living God.
ROMANS 9:26 NKJV

Hear Me, O My people, and listen to My words. You give attention continually to the words of others. You listen, read, you study and ponder and consider multitudes of words that express only the thoughts of others who, like yourself, are searching for Truth. To search is not evil, but if you desire understanding, come directly to Me. Ask of Me. As the Scriptures teaches, if any seeks wisdom, let him ask of God, for He gives liberally (James 1:5).

Wait upon Me, and I will clarify things that are dark and puzzling to you.

Whose words do I listen to?

Remove the Barriers

But to Israel he says: "All day long I have stretched
out My hands to a disobedient and
contrary people."
ROMANS 10:21 NKJV

My children, over many barriers I call to you. Man has erected walls that separate brothers, but you, My people, have allowed many walls to separate yourselves from the full revelation of My glory.

I do not withhold Myself by choice, but you prevent Me from fellowshipping with you. Curtains of doubt, fear, timidity, unrepentance, and many others hide My face from you so that you cannot know Me.

I plead with you, yes, I cry out to you that before it is too late you will turn to Me with no devices of self-defense, and then can I open My heart to you and pour out My blessings.

What walls have separated me from God?

Counsel with Me

from Progress of Another Pilgrim

(According as it is written, God hath given them
the spirit of slumber, eyes that they should not see,
and ears that they should not hear;) unto this day.

ROMANS 11:8

Be not disturbed by evildoers. They
are in My hand to do as I please,
even as are the righteous. Do not be
alarmed. All is under My control.
Stand upon My Word, and let your
only support be your faith in Me. I
Myself will hold you up and keep you
from swaying.

What goes on in the lives of others
need not distress you. I will deal with
them. Walk in Me. Counsel with Me,
and look to Me alone for your direction and your encouragement.

Go your way in peace and in rejoicing. The Lord your God is with you
and will be your helper.

Do I look to God alone for direction?

True Holiness

from *On the Highroad of Surrender*

I beseech you therefore, brethren, by the mercies
of God, that you present your bodies a living
sacrifice, holy, acceptable to God, which is your
reasonable service.

ROMANS 12:1

True holiness, when wrought in
you by My grace, is not an end
in itself. It is a transforming work by
the Holy Spirit to the end that My
will may be accomplished through
you. If you are a flowing, vital part of
My eternal purpose, you are blessed.
If you, by your willful disobedience,
become a hindering factor, you suffer
in accordance to the degree of your
rebellion.

Stretch forth the hand of faith. Set
foot upon the territory you wish to
claim. I will move ahead of you and
clear a path, but you must be determined to follow closely, and to hold
your ground without wavering.

What territory do I wish to claim?

Your Body, a Living Sacrifice

from *Come Away My Beloved*

Present your bodies a living sacrifice, holy, acceptable
unto God, which is your reasonable service. And be
not conformed to this world: but be ye transformed by the renewing of your mind,
that ye may prove what is that good,
and acceptable, and perfect, will of God.

ROMANS 12:1–2

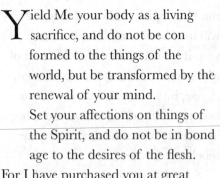

Yield Me your body as a living sacrifice, and do not be con
formed to the things of the world, but be transformed by the renewal of your mind.

Set your affections on things of the Spirit, and do not be in bond age to the desires of the flesh.

For I have purchased you at great price.

Yes, you are My special possession and My treasure.

How can I become a "living sacrifice" to God?

Return unto Me

from *Come Away My Beloved*

Do not be conformed to this world, but be
transformed by the renewing of your mind, that
you may prove what is that good and acceptable
and perfect will of God.

ROMANS 12:2 NKJV

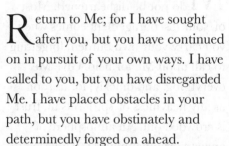

Return to Me; for I have sought
after you, but you have continued
on in pursuit of your own ways. I have
called to you, but you have disregarded
Me. I have placed obstacles in your
path, but you have obstinately and
determinedly forged on ahead.

Have you learned no wisdom? Have
past lessons fled your mind?

Put down your anxieties, and trust
Me for everything. You need nothing
but what I am fully able to supply, with
no effort on your part.

Come close to Me, and I will minister to you and revive your spirit.

*Am I conformed to God's will or
following my own?*

Anxiety

from On the Highroad of Surrender

Rejoicing in hope, patient in tribulation, continuing
steadfastly in prayer.
ROMANS 12:12 NKJV

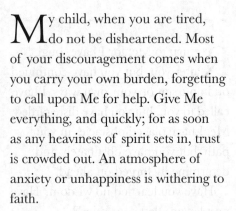

My child, when you are tired,
do not be disheartened. Most
of your discouragement comes when
you carry your own burden, forgetting
to call upon Me for help. Give Me
everything, and quickly; for as soon
as any heaviness of spirit sets in, trust
is crowded out. An atmosphere of
anxiety or unhappiness is withering to
faith.

Continual prayer will fortify your
soul.

Is anything withering my faith today?

Righteousness, Peace, and Joy

from *On the Highroad of Surrender*

For the kingdom of God is not eating and drinking,
but righteousness and peace and joy in the Holy
Spirit. For he who serves Christ in these things is
acceptable to God and approved by men.
ROMANS 14:17–18 NKJV

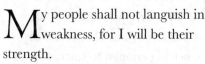

My people shall not languish in weakness, for I will be their strength.

No evil force can hold back My Spirit.

Believe Me and trust Me. You need not plot and scheme and plan. To doubt and to strive is to detain the Spirit. He needs not your help—only your submission. Give it willingly and gladly; yes, give it quickly, for the kingdom of God is righteousness, peace, and joy in the Holy Ghost, and you hinder the Spirit when these are not ruling your heart.

Am I striving or submitting?

Faith, a Perpendicular Operation

from *Progress of Another Pilgrim*

And he that doubteth is damned if he eat,
because he eateth not of faith; for whatsoever
is not of faith is sin.

ROMANS 14:23

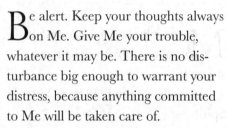

Be alert. Keep your thoughts always on Me. Give Me your trouble, whatever it may be. There is no disturbance big enough to warrant your distress, because anything committed to Me will be taken care of.

Be steadfast, and be one about whom it can be said that you truly live and walk by faith. I will be with you and help you, and I will be your strength.

No barrier shall stand in your way, because faith is a perpendicular operation. Your faith reaches straight up to Me, and My power comes straight down upon the place of action.

What troubles can I give to God today?

You Are Violating My Will

from *Progress of Another Pilgrim*

We then that are strong ought to bear the
infirmities of the weak, and not to please
ourselves. Let every one of us please his
neighbour for his good to edification.

ROMANS 15:1–2

My child, you are not where I
would have you be. How can I
be pleased with you? "Love," it is written, "seeketh not her own." But you
have been pursuing your own ends,
and this, to Me, is folly. What you
desire may be beautiful and good and
may constitute nothing that is harmful
in itself; all the same, you are violating
My will and marring My pattern.

*Are there any ways in which I'm violating
God's will in my life?*

First Place

from *Come Away My Beloved*

Even Christ pleased not himself.

ROMANS 15:3

Every soldier must give first place
to his obligation to the armed
forces, and second place to his own
private life and wishes. Even so you
must do, if you would be My followers. Even so did Jesus during His
earthly ministry. His entire life was
subordinated to the Father's will.

How dare you risk allowing the
flesh to manifest its desires? They can
be only evil continually. No good thing
can come out of a deceitful heart.

Only that generated within you
by the Spirit of God can bring forth
righteousness; do not be conformed
to this world, but be transformed by
the renewing of your mind, that you
may personally discover what is the
good and acceptable and perfect will
of God.

Am I discovering God's perfect will?

An Open Vessel

from On the Highroad of Surrender

Now may the God of hope fill you with all joy and
peace in believing, that you may abound in hope by
the power of the Holy Spirit.

ROMANS 15:13 NKJV

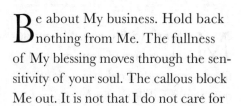

Be about My business. Hold back
nothing from Me. The fullness
of My blessing moves through the sensitivity of your soul. The callous block
Me out. It is not that I do not care for
them, but it is that I find no response.

Give Me an open vessel into which
I may pour My Spirit. Though it be of
clay, it shall overflow with glory.

*How can I open myself to receive
God's Spirit?*

August 25

Strength and Weakness

from On the Highroad of Surrender

But of Him you are in Christ Jesus, who became
for us wisdom from God—and righteousness and
sanctification and redemption—that, as it is written,
"He who glories, let him glory in the LORD."

1 CORINTHIANS 1:30–31 NKJV

M y Spirit within you, My child,
is the source of your spiritual
life and strength. Look not to your
own natural abilities, for My Spirit
empowers the one who would walk in
faith, so that he who is weak need not
despair, and he who feels himself to
be strong shall learn not to boast; for
I bring down the mighty and make
strong the weak.

*Do I look to myself or to God for my
strength?*

On the Waters of Sorrow

from Come Away My Beloved

But as it is written: "Eye has not seen,
nor ear heard, nor have entered into the heart
of man the things which God has prepared
for those who love Him."

1 CORINTHIANS 2:9 NKJV

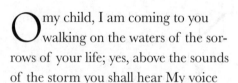

O my child, I am coming to you walking on the waters of the sorrows of your life; yes, above the sounds of the storm you shall hear My voice call your name.

You are never alone, for I am at your right hand. Never despair, for I am watching over and caring for you. Be not anxious. What seems to you to be at present a difficult situation is all part of My planning, and I am working out the details of circumstances so that I may bless you and reveal Myself to you in a new way.

What tempts me to feel despair or anxiety?

A Way of Triumph

from *Progress of Another Pilgrim*

But as it is written, Eye hath not seen,
nor ear heard, neither have entered into the
heart of man, the things which God hath prepared
for them that love him.

1 Corinthians 2:9

Never be led by human reasoning. The day is coming when you would have faltered but for the understanding I am giving you now.

It is a way of triumph when it leads to fuller enlightenment. When My presence is with you, you can know there is a blessing in store. It shall open to you as you trust Me. It shall be beautiful beyond your highest dreams.

Am I on the way of triumph?

Seek Me in the Hidden Places

from *Progress of Another Pilgrim*

But God hath revealed them unto us by his Spirit:
for the Spirit searcheth all things, yea, the deep
things of God. For what man knoweth the things
of a man, save the spirit of man which is in him?
even so the things of God knoweth no man,
but the Spirit of God.

1 CORINTHIANS 2:10–11

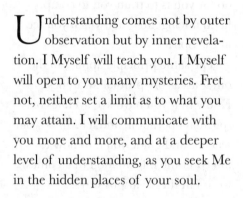

Understanding comes not by outer observation but by inner revelation. I Myself will teach you. I Myself will open to you many mysteries. Fret not, neither set a limit as to what you may attain. I will communicate with you more and more, and at a deeper level of understanding, as you seek Me in the hidden places of your soul.

How deeply do I want to communicate with God?

Spiritual Awareness

from *Progress of Another Pilgrim*

Now we have received, not the spirit of the world,
but the spirit which is of God; that we might know
the things that are freely given to us of God.

1 CORINTHIANS 2:12

As a child has eyesight, but only by teaching and study does he learn the art of reading, so likewise, what I do for you is to train you to comprehend intelligently that which you see in the Spirit.

The same principle applies in the other areas of spiritual awareness. Know that you have five avenues of spiritual operation, and let Me be your teacher and guide you into how to interpret the information that comes to you in these various ways.

Is God my only teacher and guide?

The Spiritual House

from On the Highroad of Surrender

For we are God's fellow workers; you are God's
field, you are God's building.

1 CORINTHIANS 3:9 NKJV

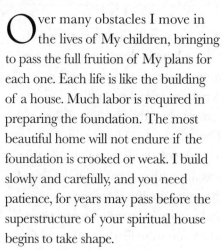

Over many obstacles I move in
the lives of My children, bringing
to pass the full fruition of My plans for
each one. Each life is like the building
of a house. Much labor is required in
preparing the foundation. The most
beautiful home will not endure if the
foundation is crooked or weak. I build
slowly and carefully, and you need
patience, for years may pass before the
superstructure of your spiritual house
begins to take shape.

The swiftness with which I build is
determined by your reception of truth.
Truth assimilated generates creativity.
Obedience practiced generates produc-
tivity. Therefore, a teachable spirit and
determined desire to do My will hastens
the working of My purposes in you.

How receptive am I to God's truth?

August 31

Share Courage

from *On the Highroad of Surrender*

To the weak I became as weak, that I might win the
weak. I have become all things to all men,
that I might by all means save some.

1 CORINTHIANS 9:22 NKJV

Your compassion for other souls
will be in direct proportion to
your own sense of need. Self-
dependence makes it difficult to
comprehend the timidity of the weak.
Though you may have gained a
measure of strength, remember that it
was not native; it has been cultivated
through a multitude of experiences,
and you can remember many times
when you were fearful and trembling.
Other souls are still in the place of
fear and desperation. Be always ready
and willing to stand with them in that
place and share your faith and courage, yes, even as many others shared
with you in your times of need!

When have I stood with the weak?

Integrity—a Sacred Charge

from *Progress of Another Pilgrim*

Whether therefore ye eat, or drink, or whatsoever
ye do, do all to the glory of God.
1 CORINTHIANS 10:31

———— ∽ ————

There is a way that you must go
because of faithfulness to Me. All
you do, let it be as unto Me. Never do
anything as pleasing men, but do all
for Me and for My glory. Thus, and
only thus, can your heart be kept at
peace, and only in this way can you
honor Me and bring forth fruit.

My Name is as perfume. Let it ever
be upon your lips. Speak of Me often,
and all other relationships shall be
hallowed.

The integrity of your own heart is
your most sacred charge. Guard this
with utmost care.

How often do I speak of Jesus?

September 2

True Dedication

from *Progress of Another Pilgrim*

But when we are judged, we are chastened of the
Lord, that we should not be condemned
with the world.

1 CORINTHIANS 11:32

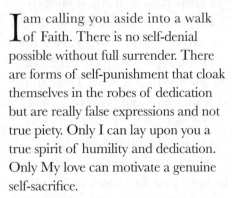

I am calling you aside into a walk of Faith. There is no self-denial possible without full surrender. There are forms of self-punishment that cloak themselves in the robes of dedication but are really false expressions and not true piety. Only I can lay upon you a true spirit of humility and dedication. Only My love can motivate a genuine self-sacrifice.

Do not deceive yourself. Let Me try your motives and probe the depths of your heart. My intention is to bless you, not to cause you unnecessary suffering.

Go your way in peace, knowing I have promised to perfect that which concerneth you, and My ways are ways of wisdom.

When has God revealed the true motives of my heart?

The Spiritual Senses

from *Progress of Another Pilgrim*

But the manifestation of the Spirit is given to every man to profit withal.

1 Corinthians 12:7

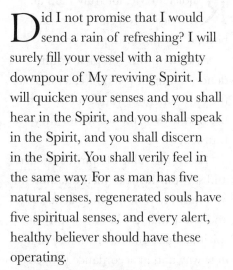

Did I not promise that I would send a rain of refreshing? I will surely fill your vessel with a mighty downpour of My reviving Spirit. I will quicken your senses and you shall hear in the Spirit, and you shall speak in the Spirit, and you shall discern in the Spirit. You shall verily feel in the same way. For as man has five natural senses, regenerated souls have five spiritual senses, and every alert, healthy believer should have these operating.

The power is given you already. Exercise it and let Me educate you along these lines.

How do I exercise the Spirit's power?

Spiritual Riches

from *On the Highroad of Surrender*

But earnestly desire the best gifts.

1 CORINTHIANS 12:31 NKJV

Rejoice in Me, for truly I am all you need. You can never ask beyond My power to provide.

Ask then, with complete confidence, but in all you desire, let it be for the enrichment of your soul. Seek not the treasures of the world, for they are transient.

Learn the value of spiritual riches, and set your heart to their attainment. You may lay your natural talents aside and know that as I bestow upon you spiritual enablements, I will use in a new way and in accordance with My highest purposes whatever lies within you of native abilities, or I may give you something entirely new. Nothing is wasted in the Spirit.

How can I seek my soul's enrichment?

The Motivation of Love

from *Progress of Another Pilgrim*

Though I speak with the tongues of men and
of angels, and have not charity, I am become as
sounding brass, or a tinkling cymbal.

1 CORINTHIANS 13:1

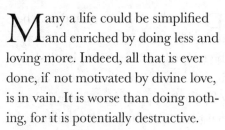

Many a life could be simplified and enriched by doing less and loving more. Indeed, all that is ever done, if not motivated by divine love, is in vain. It is worse than doing nothing, for it is potentially destructive.

There are those who have risen to fame through their noble acts, only to fall into shame and disrepute because of a bitter spirit.

Is all I do motivated by love?

Purity of Motive

from *Progress of Another Pilgrim*

Though I speak with the tongues of men and
of angels, and have not charity, I am become as
sounding brass, or a tinkling cymbal.

1 CORINTHIANS 13:1

Regardless of how sacred may be the nature of a ministry, it may be marred by a heart that is selfish or impure. Whatever does not spring out of pure love for God and love for your fellowman becomes only a hollow noise.

The work of the Kingdom suffers delay for lack of laborers; but let those who desire to serve continually offer up a yielded vessel that I may cleanse it from sin and perfect it in righteousness and fill it with love. Only thus is it possible for any man to enter into the activity of the Spirit of God in a way that furthers the divine purpose.

When has my heart been selfish or impure?

On Privacy

from *On the Highroad of Surrender*

Love suffers long and is kind; love does not envy;
love does not parade itself, is not puffed up; does
not behave rudely, does not seek its own,
is not provoked, thinks no evil.

1 CORINTHIANS 13:4–5 NKJV

———

D o not allow your thoughts to pursue in curiosity what you do not understand in the lives of others.

To violate the spiritual privacy of another is a greater breach of ethics than to invade his house uninvited. Rest assured that if your friendship warrants, he will share with you as he deems wise, and what he appears to withhold, you will (if your affection for him is genuine) have the confidence that he is withholding as much for your own good as for his.

Love believes only the best. There is no more eloquent way to express love and respect for another than by allowing him full liberty of independent action.

In what relationships do I need to protect privacy?

Flesh and Blood

from *Come Away My Beloved*

Now this I say, brethren, that flesh and blood
cannot inherit the kingdom of God; neither doth
corruption inherit incorruption.

1 CORINTHIANS 15:50

I ask you not to do, but to be.
For whatsoever is of the flesh is
flesh; but when you allow My Spirit
to have free course, then those things
that shall be accomplished both within
and through you will be truly the life
of God.

For My Spirit is the Spirit of Life,
and My Spirit is the motivating
power of Divine energy.

All else is death. As it is written,
"Flesh and blood cannot inherit the
Kingdom of God" (see 1 Corinthians
15:50).

Neither can man through any en-
deavor of his own, however holy his
purpose, produce this life, which does
not exist apart from the direct activity
of the Spirit of God.

*How freely do I allow the Spirit to
move in my life?*

I Will Bring the Victory

from *Come Away My Beloved*

Thanks be to God, who gives us the victory
through our Lord Jesus Christ.
1 CORINTHIANS 15:57 NKJV

O My child, have I ever failed you? Have I not been your refuge and your strong defense? Fear not. My purposes will be fulfilled in spite of your weaknesses, if in your need you rely on My strength.

My will shall be done regardless of the flaws in your life, if you count on the power of My righteousness. I glory in overruling the prevailing circumstances, and I take pleasure in bringing victories in those places where no victory is anywhere in sight.

Count on My coming.

Ask for the victory. I will come and bring it.

How often do I ask God for the victory?

The Course Lies
Dead Ahead

from *Progress of Another Pilgrim*

But thanks be to God, which giveth us the victory
through our Lord Jesus Christ.

1 CORINTHIANS 15:57

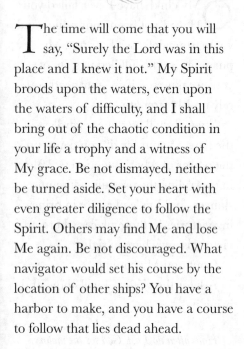

The time will come that you will say, "Surely the Lord was in this place and I knew it not." My Spirit broods upon the waters, even upon the waters of difficulty, and I shall bring out of the chaotic condition in your life a trophy and a witness of My grace. Be not dismayed, neither be turned aside. Set your heart with even greater diligence to follow the Spirit. Others may find Me and lose Me again. Be not discouraged. What navigator would set his course by the location of other ships? You have a harbor to make, and you have a course to follow that lies dead ahead.

Is my course set on God or other ships?

The Door Is Open

from *On the Highroad of Surrender*

*For a great and effective door has opened to me,
and there are many adversaries.*

1 CORINTHIANS 16:9 NKJV

My child, the door is open. You shall go through by My grace and in My strength. Never gauge the possibilities of victory by examining your own strength. I am your Life, your Purity, your Wisdom, and your Strength. You have built faith for many years through a knowledge of and confidence in My Word. Now, I say unto you, Put it into operation by walking in the path of action. Only in this way can you come into the full possession of your inheritance.

Move out, and trust Me as you go.

Give Me your yieldedness, your love, and a pure desire. I will do the rest.

What door has God opened for me? Am I ready to walk through it?

A Way-Preparer

from *Progress of Another Pilgrim*

Watch ye, stand fast in the faith,
quit you like men, be strong.

1 CORINTHIANS 16:13

———————⚬———————

Be tolerant of all, at whatever stage of spiritual development they may be, but do not set your standards by theirs. I am moving, and I want you to be a way-preparer. Get into the front ranks, and hold your position. Never flinch. Certainly I can expect you never to turn coward and flee!

Give Me the privilege of sustaining you in the dangerous position. Think you not that I am well able to keep you there and adequately supply every needed grace?

How willing am I to step into God's
front ranks?

Recognition and Focus

from On the Highroad of Surrender

But we all, with unveiled face, beholding as in a
mirror the glory of the Lord, are being transformed
into the same image from glory to glory, just as by
the Spirit of the Lord.

2 CORINTHIANS 3:18 NKJV

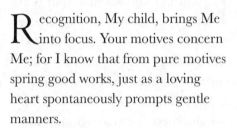

Recognition, My child, brings Me into focus. Your motives concern Me; for I know that from pure motives spring good works, just as a loving heart spontaneously prompts gentle manners.

Recognition is the sight I give your inner eye to discern distortion of My image in your own character. I do not say in your brother's, but in your own! I would have your personality patterns display My character, and wherever this fails to be so, there is distortion of the image, and as others look to you for guidance and inspiration, they do not see a clear image of Me.

How do others see God when they look at me?

Boundless Joy

from *Progress of Another Pilgrim*

But we have this treasure in earthen vessels,
that the excellency of the power may be of God,
and not of us.

2 CORINTHIANS 4:7

———————— ⌘ ————————

Know in your heart that your vessel has been formed for the purpose of shedding abroad the glory of God, and the Spirit ministers in you to the end that this may be accomplished.

Lo, I stand at your side to help, and you shall never need to rely on your own strength or wisdom. As long as you bless and honor Me, the rivers of life shall flow forth and your joy shall be boundless.

How am I blessing and honoring God?

Saturate Your Soul in the Oil of the Spirit

from *Come Away My Beloved*

We are hard-pressed on every side, yet not
crushed; we are perplexed, but not in despair;
persecuted, but not forsaken.

2 CORINTHIANS 4:8–9 NKJV

━━━━━━━━ ∾ ━━━━━━━━

The everlasting power of the God-head is incarnate in My chosen ones. Is it not written that the kingdom of God dwells within you? I will bring to pass miracles—when you walk in uprightness and with mercy.

Come to Me with a clean heart and a right spirit, in sincerity, in honesty. Sin brings forth death; and any negative current flowing within your body will produce a steady regression.

Saturate your soul in the oil of the Holy Spirit, and keep your channel of communication always open to your Heavenly Father.

*How clean is my heart—and how right
is my spirit?*

Thorns in the Nest

from *Progress of Another Pilgrim*

For our light affliction, which is but for a moment,
worketh for us a far more exceeding and eternal
weight of glory.

2 CORINTHIANS 4:17

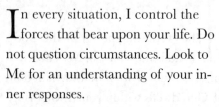

In every situation, I control the forces that bear upon your life. Do not question circumstances. Look to Me for an understanding of your inner responses.

Man looks upon the natural, physical world: My concern is for your spiritual life, that virtues may develop in you. While you are praying for a problem to be solved, a need to be met, a thorn to be removed from your nest, I am watching for true faith to express in the time of want, and I am waiting to see when the thorns in the nest will cause you to move out and try your unused wings.

When have I tried my spiritual "wings"?

Grief

from On the Highroad of Surrender

For our light affliction, which is but for a moment,
is working for us a far more exceeding and eternal
weight of glory.

2 CORINTHIANS 4:17 NKJV

Behold, there is a river of divine grace flowing beneath all your need. Under your deepest sorrow moves My compassion and My love. In a very real sense, you fathom the depth of My own heart only to the extent that your heart is broken and your inmost consciousness torn asunder by the pain of grief.

All things to grow require a proper climate. Love, if it is to be given, must also be received. You are never so ready to accept My love as when you are experiencing anguish.

Never look upon trials and tests and disciplines as being damaging. Whatever hurt they seem to bring is outweighed by the blessing that follows.

When have I sought God's grace in grief?

September 18

Blessing in Adversity

from *Come Away My Beloved*

For our light affliction, which is but for a moment,
worketh for us a far more exceeding and eternal
weight of glory.
2 Corinthians 4:17

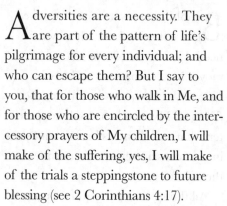

A dversities are a necessity. They are part of the pattern of life's pilgrimage for every individual; and who can escape them? But I say to you, that for those who walk in Me, and for those who are encircled by the intercessory prayers of My children, I will make of the suffering, yes, I will make of the trials a steppingstone to future blessing (see 2 Corinthians 4:17).

My arms are around you, and never have I loved you more! I will make you like a garden of fountains whose streams are fed by the mountain springs.

Am I looking at my trials or forward to God's blessing?

The Law of Plenty

from *On the Highroad of Surrender*

As poor, yet making many rich; as having nothing,
and yet possessing all things.

2 CORINTHIANS 6:10

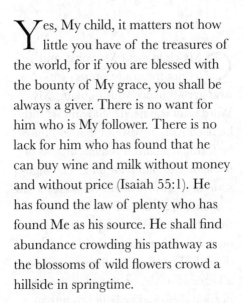

Yes, My child, it matters not how little you have of the treasures of the world, for if you are blessed with the bounty of My grace, you shall be always a giver. There is no want for him who is My follower. There is no lack for him who has found that he can buy wine and milk without money and without price (Isaiah 55:1). He has found the law of plenty who has found Me as his source. He shall find abundance crowding his pathway as the blossoms of wild flowers crowd a hillside in springtime.

What kind of abundance crowds my path?

September 20

Recognize the Enemy

from *On the Highroad of Surrender*

Do not be unequally yoked together with
unbelievers. For what fellowship has righteousness
with lawlessness? And what communion has
light with darkness?

2 CORINTHIANS 6:14 NKJV

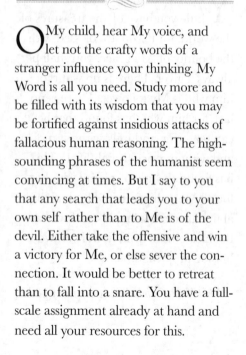

O My child, hear My voice, and
let not the crafty words of a
stranger influence your thinking. My
Word is all you need. Study more and
be filled with its wisdom that you may
be fortified against insidious attacks of
fallacious human reasoning. The high-
sounding phrases of the humanist seem
convincing at times. But I say to you
that any search that leads you to your
own self rather than to Me is of the
devil. Either take the offensive and win
a victory for Me, or else sever the con-
nection. It would be better to retreat
than to fall into a snare. You have a full-
scale assignment already at hand and
need all your resources for this.

What crafty words have distracted me
from God's will?

No Compromise!

from On the Highroad of Surrender

Wherefore come out from among them, and be ye separate, saith the Lord, and touch not the unclean thing; and I will receive you.

2 CORINTHIANS 6:17

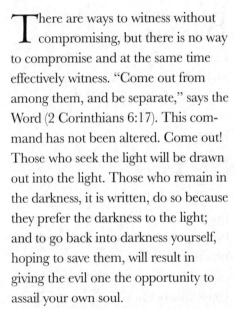

There are ways to witness without compromising, but there is no way to compromise and at the same time effectively witness. "Come out from among them, and be separate," says the Word (2 Corinthians 6:17). This command has not been altered. Come out! Those who seek the light will be drawn out into the light. Those who remain in the darkness, it is written, do so because they prefer the darkness to the light; and to go back into darkness yourself, hoping to save them, will result in giving the evil one the opportunity to assail your own soul.

You cannot have both—light and darkness—for "what accord has Christ with Belial?" (2 Corinthians 6:14–18).

Am I separate or compromised?

Brokenness

from *On the Highroad of Surrender*

For godly sorrow produces repentance leading to
salvation, not to be regretted; but the sorrow of the
world produces death.

2 CORINTHIANS 7:10 NKJV

———— ⟨≈⟩ ————

Brokenness comes only by the hand of the Holy Spirit upon the human heart. The storms of life may make shipwreck of a soul, but this may be purely destructive. The brokenness of spirit wrought by the hand of God becomes a constructive work. It is the godly sorrow unto repentance that brings Life.

The soul abounds in grace when prayer is its breath, and true prayer is born out of brokenness. This brokenness is contrition for sins, tenderness of feeling, and gratitude for grace. If you let it work in your heart, it will surely draw you closer and closer to Me.

*When have I experienced true
brokenness?*

The Larger Life

from *Progress of Another Pilgrim*

And he said unto me, My grace is sufficient for thee:
for my strength is made perfect in weakness. Most
gladly therefore will I rather glory in my infirmities,
that the power of Christ may rest upon me.

2 CORINTHIANS 12:9

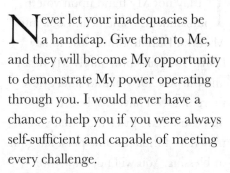

Never let your inadequacies be a handicap. Give them to Me, and they will become My opportunity to demonstrate My power operating through you. I would never have a chance to help you if you were always self-sufficient and capable of meeting every challenge.

Be ready to move in faith every time you sense inadequacy, and in each experience, as you trust Me, you will experience what is meant by "the larger life." I will fill all your lack with My divine undertaking and bring you out with a testimony unto My Name.

What personal inadequacies can I give to God today?

September 24

A Consuming Desire

from *On the Highroad of Surrender*

For do I now persuade men, or God? Or do I seek
to please men? For if I still pleased men, I would
not be a bondservant of Christ.

GALATIANS 1:10 NKJV

If I lay not My hand upon you in punishment, come near. Look into My eyes. Dare to draw close to My heart. You will know surely My desire and purpose for you and shall grieve more that you have displeased Me and caused Me grief than that you may have forfeited some personal gain or blessing. You will not view your spiritual walk as a challenge to be a successful Christian in the eyes of others, but will have a consuming desire to please Me and bring only joy to My heart.

Whose approval do I seek in my
Christian life?

Look Deeply

from Progress of Another Pilgrim

But I certify you, brethren, that the gospel which
was preached of me is not after man. For I neither
received it of man, neither was I taught it, but by
the revelation of Jesus Christ.

<small>GALATIANS 1:11–12</small>

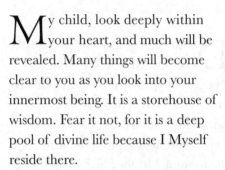

M y child, look deeply within
your heart, and much will be
revealed. Many things will become
clear to you as you look into your
innermost being. It is a storehouse of
wisdom. Fear it not, for it is a deep
pool of divine life because I Myself
reside there.

I will teach you in symbols as you
learn to see in the Spirit.

Dismiss traditions. You disdain
them but you still allow yourself to be
held in bondage to them. Drive out
the bondman. Your spirit needs free
course for expression. Do not hamper
it in ignorance.

*Does tradition bind me, or am I free in
God's Spirit?*

I Anticipate Your Dependence on Me

from *Come Away My Beloved*

I have been crucified with Christ; it is no longer I who live, but Christ lives in me; and the life which I now live in the flesh I live by faith in the Son of God, who loved me and gave Himself for me.

GALATIANS 2:20 NKJV

———— ⟡ ————

Do not wait to feel worthy, for no one is worthy of My blessings. My grace bypasses your shortcomings, and I give to My children because they ask of Me and because I love them. I give most liberally to those who ask the most of Me, for I love to have you depend on Me. As your Father, I anticipate your dependence on Me.

As you open your heart to Me, I will come to you. As you speak to Me, I will speak to you. As you reveal yourself to Me, I will reveal Myself to you.

How completely do I depend on God?

I Must Have Overcomers

from Come Away My Beloved

I have been crucified with Christ. . .the life which
I now live in the flesh I live by faith in the Son of
God, who loved me and gave Himself for me.
GALATIANS 2:20 NKJV

O My children, the path where I
will lead you is not a pleasant
way, nor in accord with your selfish
desires.

You have faith in Me; this is good,
but faith without works is dead.

I must have overcomers through
whom I may overcome. There is an
enemy to be contested and defeated.
My new life will become yours in
direct proportion to your success in
emptying your heart of self-will.

I know you cannot do this for yourself; but you must will it to be done.
And as you will it, I will work with you
and within you to bring it to pass.

*What works have shown that my faith
is real?*

Ionospheric Christian Living

from *Progress of Another Pilgrim*

Stand fast therefore in the liberty wherewith Christ
hath made us free, and be not entangled again with
the yoke of bondage.

GALATIANS 5:1

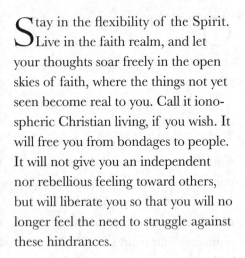

Stay in the flexibility of the Spirit.
Live in the faith realm, and let
your thoughts soar freely in the open
skies of faith, where the things not yet
seen become real to you. Call it iono-
spheric Christian living, if you wish. It
will free you from bondages to people.
It will not give you an independent
nor rebellious feeling toward others,
but will liberate you so that you will no
longer feel the need to struggle against
these hindrances.

How free is my Christian life?

The Disciplines of Freedom

from *On the Highroad of Surrender*

Stand fast therefore in the liberty by which Christ
has made us free, and do not be entangled again
with a yoke of bondage.

GALATIANS 5:1 NKJV

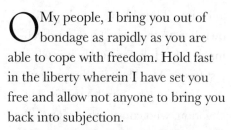

O My people, I bring you out of bondage as rapidly as you are able to cope with freedom. Hold fast in the liberty wherein I have set you free and allow not anyone to bring you back into subjection.

All sin is binding. In Christ is freedom, because in Him is holiness. Your constant desire for purity is your safeguard against the desire to return to the fleshpots and the slavery of Egypt, which is always a symbol of the world. The world with its desires passes away, but he who chooses to do the will of God will live forever.

Am I standing fast in His freedom?

Magnificent Gift

from Dialogues with God

This I say then, Walk in the Spirit, and ye shall not
fulfil the lust of the flesh.

GALATIANS 5:16

W ell I know the instability of
the human heart and natural
affection. Thus I have supplied My
own love to thy heart by the indwelling of My Holy Spirit. He it is who
testifies of Me. He it is who prompts
thy worship, who kindles the fires of
devotion, who constantly draweth thee
to Myself. For the carnal nature is hos-
tile toward God, but the Holy Spirit
within you ever crieth "Abba, Father,"
and He shall glorify Me at all times
(Galatians 4:6, John 16:14).

Do ye long to love Me more deeply?
Seek the infilling of My Holy Spirit. In
this one magnificent gift, I have made
full provision for thine every need.

*What do I need the Spirit to help me
with today?*

Pride

from On the Highroad of Surrender

For the flesh lusts against the Spirit, and the
Spirit against the flesh; and these are contrary to
one another, so that you do not do the things
that you wish.

GALATIANS 5:17 NKJV

Stand firm in your convictions
against the contrary wind. Every
soul struggles against the elements.
Thoughts of others can come upon
you like a storm at sea until your boat
is well-near swamped. Except for My
grace, it would be destroyed. But I am
near at hand. Purify your heart so that
I can be glorified in all your thoughts
and actions.

I am concerned for your victory.
You may have it as you fall back into
My arms and cease struggling.

Guard your heart from false values,
and beware when man begins to
scheme and promote. I am not in it,
says the Lord.

How firm are my convictions?

Grow Up in Me

from *Come Away My Beloved*

The fruit of the Spirit is love, joy, peace,
longsuffering, kindness, goodness, faithfulness,
gentleness, self-control.

GALATIANS 5:22–23 NKJV

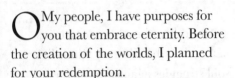

O My people, I have purposes for
you that embrace eternity. Before
the creation of the worlds, I planned
for your redemption.

Now that you are in Christ, you have
My life abiding in you, and you have
become a new creation. Grow up in
Me now, so that you may develop into
the full stature of men and women—
even to the measure of the fullness of
Christ (see Ephesians 4:13).

My purpose was not simply to bring
you into My family to remain as babies
or children. I am concerned with your
maturity; with your growth in wisdom
and knowledge of things pertaining
to Myself; with the perfection of your
ministry; and with the producing of the
fruits of the Spirit in your life.

Where do I stand in spiritual maturity?

The Fruits of the Spirit

from *Progress of Another Pilgrim*

The fruit of the Spirit is love, joy, peace,
longsuffering, kindness, goodness, faithfulness,
gentleness, self-control.
GALATIANS 5:22–23 NKJV

My little children, I would speak to you concerning the fruits of the Spirit. I would have you understand how My presence within you, My divine life, operating in your human heart, creates the fruits of the Spirit.

It is not by self-effort that these heavenly attributes are brought forth. Verily, the fruits of the Spirit are not native to the world. The carnal man never brings forth this fruit.

Love, joy, and peace: these were natural to Jesus, but they are foreign to man's fallen nature. You will never produce them by seeking to suppress evil emotions. I am able to bring them forth even from your inmost being as you allow Me to live in you.

What spiritual fruit has grown in my life?

The Centrifugal Power of the Holy Spirit

from *Progress of Another Pilgrim*

But the fruit of the Spirit is love, joy, peace, long-suffering, gentleness, goodness, faith, meekness, temperance: against such there is no law.

GALATIANS 5:22–23

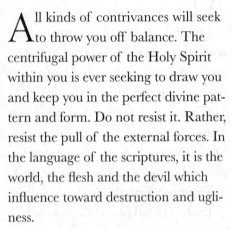

All kinds of contrivances will seek to throw you off balance. The centrifugal power of the Holy Spirit within you is ever seeking to draw you and keep you in the perfect divine pattern and form. Do not resist it. Rather, resist the pull of the external forces. In the language of the scriptures, it is the world, the flesh and the devil which influence toward destruction and ugliness.

Only the divine Spirit of God—nothing else—can preserve your soul and life in the beauty of purity and the expression of grace.

Are purity and grace hallmarks of my life?

Set Your Heart to Follow to the End

from Come Away My Beloved

For he who sows to his flesh will of the flesh reap
corruption, but he who sows to the Spirit will of
the Spirit reap everlasting life.

GALATIANS 6:8 NKJV

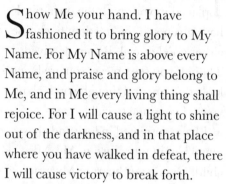

Show Me your hand. I have fashioned it to bring glory to My Name. For My Name is above every Name, and praise and glory belong to Me, and in Me every living thing shall rejoice. For I will cause a light to shine out of the darkness, and in that place where you have walked in defeat, there I will cause victory to break forth.

Rise, arise, and put on your strength, for you are a people called by My Name, and in My Name you will be strong and accomplish great things. And I will bless you out of the abundance of heaven.

My strength shall be your delivering power.

Where have I walked in defeat?

October 6

Holiness upon the Heart

from *On the Highroad of Surrender*

Just as He chose us in Him before the foundation
of the world, that we should be holy and without
blame before Him in love.

EPHESIANS 1:4 NKJV

I the Lord have tried you. I have
placed in your path the open pit. I
have given you the freedom to choose
either good or evil. Be not deceived.
Though you see no eye, you are being
looked upon, and though you seek no
voice, I continue to call.

I have entreated in love and chastened you in pity. Turn to Me, My
child. Open your heart to My grace.

Holiness shall be written upon
the hearts of My people. They shall
minister in power because they live in
obedience, and if any do not desire
obedience and discipline, he shall not
be My disciple.

How open is my heart to God's grace?

Soul's Rest

from *Come Away My Beloved*

And [God] hath raised us up together, and made
us sit together in heavenly places in Christ Jesus.
EPHESIANS 2:6

Bring Me all that puzzles you.
Many questions need no answer,
for when the heart is at one with the
Father, there comes an illumination of
Spirit that transcends thought.

Learn to worship and you will have
rest of soul; you will rise to a new
place of fellowship, where you will be
made to "sit together in the heavenly
places in Christ Jesus."

You will be taught by the Spirit.
Yes, He will open the mysteries of the
Word to you. For it was by the Spirit
of God that the Scriptures were given
to holy men of old; even so, by the
Spirit will the treasures of the Word be
revealed to you.

How often do I hear the Spirit's voice?

October 8

Folly of Immaturity

from *On the Highroad of Surrender*

And that you put on the new man which was created
according to God, in true righteousness and holiness.
EPHESIANS 4:24 NKJV

It is so simple when you approach
Me in proper fashion and do not
hinder your spiritual progress by
regression to a parent-child position
in your attitude. I know full well when
you are no longer properly in that
stage, and although you may attempt
to fall back into it to avoid responsibility, I will not respond, and you will be
left to a folly of your own making.

When have I fallen into immaturity?

The Importance of Time and Kindness

from *Progress of Another Pilgrim*

Be ye therefore followers of God, as dear children;
And walk in love, as Christ also hath loved us, and
hath given himself for us an offering and a sacrifice
to God for a sweetsmelling savour.

EPHESIANS 5:1–2

Time is of supreme importance. Waste none. Let Me help you know what is worthy of attention and what is not; otherwise you may be tempted to eliminate the things I most desire you to do.

Having a schedule will help you, but remember that kindness is more indicative of spiritual fervor than all your efficiency in work. Never let your works of righteousness crowd out the little acts of thoughtfulness. The labors of the hands must never take precedence over the gentle expressions of a compassionate heart.

Am I both righteous and thoughtful?

Speak the Truth

from *Come Away My Beloved*

Finally, my brethren, be strong in the Lord and in
the power of his might.

EPHESIANS 6:10

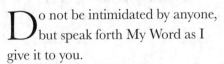

Do not be intimidated by anyone, but speak forth My Word as I give it to you.

You are not pleasing Me but trying to please men. They will detect your inconsistency in spite of your best efforts, for in one way or another, the truth will break through. You need not say all that is in your heart, but you must either speak the truth or be silent. If you cannot bring yourself to speak the truth without apology, then speak nothing.

Let the life and witness of Jesus Christ be your guide.

Am I speaking the truth without apology?

The Mystery of Righteousness

from *On the Highroad of Surrender*

For we do not wrestle against flesh and blood, but
against principalities, against powers, against the
rulers of the darkness of this age, against spiritual
hosts of wickedness in the heavenly places.

EPHESIANS 6:12 NKJV

Grace is My abundant mercies showered upon the spiritually destitute. It is the fullness of My love poured out upon the loveless. Return unto Me, and I will forgive your iniquities and heal your backslidings.

There is no peace in the heart of the transgressor and no joy in his spirit. But though you leave Me, I have not left you. With your own hands you have made for your soul a shack. I have prepared for you a mansion. You have chosen death, but I have chosen for you life in its abundance.

Do not faint, My child, and do not forsake the way of the Spirit for the way of the flesh.

What backslidings do I need to confess?

October 12

Concentration

from *On the Highroad of Surrender*

For we do not wrestle against flesh and blood, but
against principalities, against powers, against the
rulers of the darkness of this age, against spiritual
hosts of wickedness in the heavenly places.

EPHESIANS 6:12 NKJV

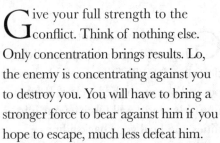

Give your full strength to the
conflict. Think of nothing else.
Only concentration brings results. Lo,
the enemy is concentrating against you
to destroy you. You will have to bring a
stronger force to bear against him if you
hope to escape, much less defeat him.

Gird on your armor, for the battle
is not against flesh and blood, but
against principalities and powers and
against spiritual forces of darkness
intruding into sacred places. I am at
your side to help you.

What spiritual battles am I currently facing?

The Power of Holiness

from On the Highroad of Surrender

For we do not wrestle against flesh and blood, but against principalities, against powers, against the rulers of the darkness of this age, against spiritual hosts of wickedness in the heavenly places.

EPHESIANS 6:12 NKJV

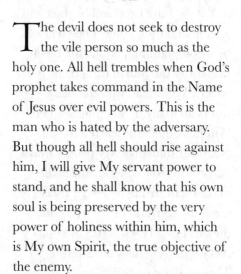

The devil does not seek to destroy the vile person so much as the holy one. All hell trembles when God's prophet takes command in the Name of Jesus over evil powers. This is the man who is hated by the adversary. But though all hell should rise against him, I will give My servant power to stand, and he shall know that his own soul is being preserved by the very power of holiness within him, which is My own Spirit, the true objective of the enemy.

It is not written that "He who is with you is greater than he who is in the world?"

What evil can I battle in Jesus' name?

Courage

from *Come Away My Beloved*

And take the helmet of salvation, and the sword of
the Spirit, which is the word of God.

EPHESIANS 6:17

My people shall not go mourning, for I the Lord will be their re-joicing and their song. They will not be a complaining people, for I will take away the murmuring from your streets. Will I lead into the battle-fronts an army of weeping women? Will I ask the fainthearted to war? No, but I shall give My people brave and courageous spirits, and I will make them strong of heart. I will give them the spirit of the martyrs, for they will be My witnesses of resurrection power. They shall be stalwart. They shall be steadfast.

So take upon you the full armor of God.

Have I put on His full armor?

Perseverance, the Angel of Love

from *On the Highroad of Surrender*

Praying always with all prayer and supplication
in the Spirit, being watchful to this end with all
perseverance and supplication for all the saints.

EPHESIANS 6:18 NKJV

Perseverance is the rope that ties the soul to the doorpost of heaven. Without it even the most pious will fail. With it, the most stupid attain.

Not to give up in face of the impossible is humanity's ultimate salvation. It is well called "the perseverance of the saints," for it requires saintly determination to continue on in dedication when all the forces of hell are arrayed against the soul.

Perseverance is to the human spirit what the rudder is to a ship. It will steer the ship dead ahead in spite of the contrary wind.

This you must have, my child. . .not fleshly zeal, but holy determination, pressing on in defiance of all odds.

How is my perseverance?

My Words Cannot Wait

from *On the Highroad of Surrender*

Being confident of this very thing, that He who has
begun a good work in you will complete it until
the day of Jesus Christ.

<small>PHILIPPIANS 1:6 NKJV</small>

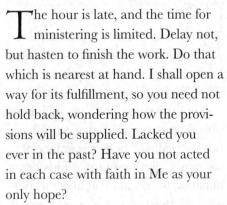

The hour is late, and the time for ministering is limited. Delay not, but hasten to finish the work. Do that which is nearest at hand. I shall open a way for its fulfillment, so you need not hold back, wondering how the provisions will be supplied. Lacked you ever in the past? Have you not acted in each case with faith in Me as your only hope?

My words cannot wait; but you have held them as though you thought the future would wait. Up! Delay no more. Obey Me, and do so quickly. Look directly to Me. I will empower and I will make all things possible as you move in obedience.

Who should I minister to today?

The Call of the Spirit

from On the Highroad of Surrender

Therefore, my beloved, as you have always obeyed,
not as in my presence only, but now much more
in my absence, work out your own salvation with
fear and trembling; for it is God who works in you
both to will and to do for His good pleasure.

PHILIPPIANS 2:12–13 NKJV

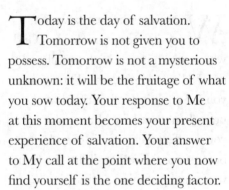

Today is the day of salvation.
Tomorrow is not given you to
possess. Tomorrow is not a mysterious
unknown: it will be the fruitage of what
you sow today. Your response to Me
at this moment becomes your present
experience of salvation. Your answer
to My call at the point where you now
find yourself is the one deciding factor.

Regret weakens, and procrastination destroys the vision.

Repent. With a whole heart seek
my face and My forgiveness. Grace
will be given according to the depth of
your confession of need.

*What needs do I need to confess to
God today?*

October 18

Salvation

from *Progress of Another Pilgrim*

Wherefore, my beloved, as ye have always obeyed,
not as in my presence only, but now much more in
my absence, work out your own salvation with fear
and trembling. For it is God which worketh in you
both to will and to do of his good pleasure.

PHILIPPIANS 2:12–13

Work out your own salvation, says the scripture, for it is God who worketh in you both to will and to do of His good pleasure. Thus, when you are conscious of spiritual weakness, do not wait for Me to move upon you to effect a change from without, but assume the responsibility for your weakened condition as though you were indeed your own savior. In the self-same moment, My grace will do the rest!

Wholeness is the product of the Spirit, but it cannot come until your own desire sets it in motion.

How am I working out my salvation?

Vision Versus Dreams

from *On the Highroad of Surrender*

Yet indeed I also count all things loss for the
excellence of the knowledge of Christ Jesus my
Lord, for whom I have suffered the loss of all
things, and count them as rubbish, that I
may gain Christ.

PHILIPPIANS 3:8 NKJV

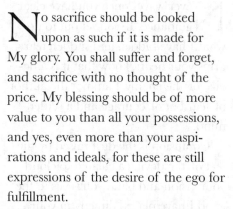

No sacrifice should be looked
upon as such if it is made for
My glory. You shall suffer and forget,
and sacrifice with no thought of the
price. My blessing should be of more
value to you than all your possessions,
and yes, even more than your aspirations and ideals, for these are still
expressions of the desire of the ego for
fulfillment.

In My Spirit there can be no
cherishing of personal dreams. Only
the doing of the Father's will is to be
sought, and there is a vast difference
between a God-inspired vision and
personal dreams and aspirations.

Do I have visions or dreams?

Forewarned and Forearmed

from *On the Highroad of Surrender*

Not that I have already attained, or am already
perfected; but I press on, that I may lay hold of
that for which Christ Jesus has also laid hold of me.

PHILIPPIANS 3:12 NKJV

———————— ∽ ————————

Never waver once you have clear
guidance. If you set out to do
what I have bidden and sudden fear
grips your heart, know that it is a device of the enemy. I am not the author
of fear but of courage and a settled
mind.

Confusion is the dust raised by the
feet of the devil, calculated to cloud
your vision and blind your eyes to the
good I have placed directly in your
path, and which you will surely find if
you continue to act in faith.

Am I wavering or standing firm in Jesus?

Communication

from Progress of Another Pilgrim

Brethren, I count not myself to have apprehended:
but this one thing I do, forgetting those things
which are behind, and reaching forth unto those
things which are before, press toward the mark for
the prize of the high calling of God in Christ Jesus.

PHILIPPIANS 3:13–14

Keep in vital communication with Me. Loose yourself from the world at every possible point. You can fulfill My purpose only when your channel is completely open and free to Me. Resist every hindrance. Yield to Me the deepest place in your consciousness. Only in this way do I have full control of your life energies. Otherwise you dissipate them in ignorance, unintentionally. I will preserve them for the Spirit's activity as you abide in the place of communion.

Do not look for any other secret of spiritual power. There is none.

How can I keep that vital line of communication open?

October 22

Press On

from *On the Highroad of Surrender*

*I press toward the goal for the prize of the high
calling of God in Christ Jesus.*

PHILIPPIANS 3:14 NKJV

O My child, you have crossed a bridge. Reach not back. Move on ahead and press into the fullness of all I have prepared for you. It is the blossoming of that which long ago was planted and for many years has been nurtured. It is waiting for you to step forward and receive. Do not tarry, and do not question, neither allow doubts to enter your mind. Your heart may cry out and rebel, but if you will turn to Me in those moments, I will give you My peace. I send you no place except as I have gone before.

Where is God sending me?

Ministering Angels

from *Come Away My Beloved*

Be anxious for nothing, but in everything by prayer
and supplication, with thanksgiving, let your
requests be made known to God.

PHILIPPIANS 4:6 NKJV

B e anxious for nothing. It is
enough that I love you. I take
thought of your smallest need. Surely
I will not allow you to be put to shame
and will not be unconcerned when
you are in any kind of need.

Always turn to Me before you look
to any other source of assistance. My
love will light your path, so that you
may be guided in finding other help.
I have given you ministering angels,
who may sometimes come to you in
the form of your friends. Accept their
help as from Me, and your blessing
will be doubled. You may also, in turn,
be used in similar manner to bless
others.

*What "other source of assistance" am I
tempted to turn to?*

You Shall Move Swiftly

from *Come Away My Beloved*

Be anxious for nothing, but in everything by prayer
and supplication, with thanksgiving, let your
requests be made known to God.

PHILIPPIANS 4:6 NKJV

I will make My will known to you,
and you will no longer move halt-
ingly, you shall move swiftly and surely.
You may not know what I am doing as
yet, but you will know hereafter, and
you will be moved by My divine unction and authority.

You will not be left to falter as a
blind man searches out his way; with
your hand in Mine, we will move
together. My Spirit will be apparent
by your life and testimony, and you
will be empowered by My might and
power.

Be anxious for nothing, but in all
situations in prayer and in fasting,
bring each emergency case to Me, for
I am the Great Physician.

How swiftly do I move to do His will?

Hesitation

from *On the Highroad of Surrender*

I can do all things through Christ
who strengthens me.
PHILIPPIANS 4:13 NKJV

Never delay My blessing by
indecision. I can only fill that
which you give Me. If you do not act
in response to My directives, you will
never receive My enablement.

I give you strength according to
the task, but I give it as you do the
work. To hesitate is to become still
more weak and timid, for it is a sense
of inadequacy that causes you to draw
back and fear to move, and this draws
your attention to yourself; and because
there is never sufficient power within
yourself to do the Father's work, any
focus on your own strength or ability
will soon persuade you that the task is
impossible.

Am I doing the work God called me to?

Provision

from *On the Highroad of Surrender*

And my God shall supply all your need according
to His riches in glory by Christ Jesus.
PHILIPPIANS 4:19 NKJV

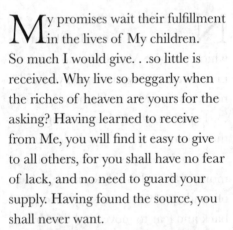

My promises wait their fulfillment in the lives of My children. So much I would give. . .so little is received. Why live so beggarly when the riches of heaven are yours for the asking? Having learned to receive from Me, you will find it easy to give to all others, for you shall have no fear of lack, and no need to guard your supply. Having found the source, you shall never want.

David's heart was freed to sing, "The Lord is my shepherd," having come to know Him as his provider. Rejoice, My children, and walk in the freedom of My abundance, looking not to others, but to Me for all things.

How easy is it for me to give to others?

Good and Evil

from On the Highroad of Surrender

That you may walk worthy of the Lord, fully
pleasing Him, being fruitful in every good work
and increasing in the knowledge of God.

COLOSSIANS 1:10 NKJV

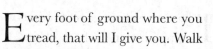

Every foot of ground where you
tread, that will I give you. Walk
in faith, and I will reward you with an
abundance of fruit.

It is not in your heart to discern
your own way. Much that is evil you
call good, and much that is good you
curse because you will bless what you
enjoy and condemn what gives you
displeasure.

I say unto you, My hand does not
always deal joy. Joy may come in the
end, but the initial action may bring
pain. Fear not. I am not only wise but
kind, and today's grief may become
the channel for tomorrow's blessing.

What blessings may come of today's griefs?

Sufferings Ahead

from *Come Away My Beloved*

Who now rejoice in my sufferings for you, and fill
up that which is behind of the afflictions of Christ
in my flesh for his body's sake, which is the church.

COLOSSIANS 1:24

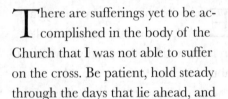

There are sufferings yet to be accomplished in the body of the
Church that I was not able to suffer
on the cross. Be patient, hold steady
through the days that lie ahead, and
know that the trials and suffering are
working toward a consuming glory.

Praise Me out of a heart full of
love. Praise Me for every blessing and
every victory. Yes, praise Me when the
most difficult thing to do is to praise.
This is the victory that overcomes the
world, even your faith, and praise is
the voice of faith.

How steady am I in suffering?

Tribulation and Stamina

from *Make Haste My Beloved*

To whom God would make known what is the
riches of the glory of this mystery among the
Gentiles; which is Christ in you, the hope of glory.

COLOSSIANS 1:27

───────────── ❦ ─────────────

Only through much prayer can
you endure much tribulation. In
no other way can the new life in Christ
develop and gain stamina.

Be as a child and trust Me implicitly.
I will honor your faith and will give
you still more.

Do not place restrictions on divine
aid by trying to live the Christian life
in your own strength. I Myself am
your victory. My kingdom shall be forever, but even now it is in your heart
whenever you bow to Me as sovereign.

Is Christ truly my victory?

Take the Glory with You

from *Come Away My Beloved*

Not holding fast to the Head, from whom
all the body, nourished and knit together by
joints and ligaments, grows with the increase that
is from God.

COLOSSIANS 2:19 NKJV

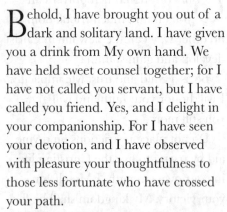

Behold, I have brought you out of a dark and solitary land. I have given you a drink from My own hand. We have held sweet counsel together; for I have not called you servant, but I have called you friend. Yes, and I delight in your companionship. For I have seen your devotion, and I have observed with pleasure your thoughtfulness to those less fortunate who have crossed your path.

Take the glory of the mountain-top with you; take My presence, My light, My love. This is not the valley of personal darkness—this is the valley where you will find those who need the touch of blessing you can bring.

How am I sharing that touch of blessing?

Fight Discouragement

from *Progress of Another Pilgrim*

If ye then be risen with Christ, seek those things
which are above, where Christ sitteth on the right
hand of God. Set your affection on things above,
not on things on the earth.

COLOSSIANS 3:1–2

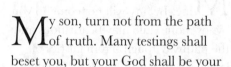

My son, turn not from the path
of truth. Many testings shall
beset you, but your God shall be your
refuge.

Open wide your soul, and the Lord
will fill it with His goodness. Your
heart shall drink in His mercy and
love; for His ear is attuned to your cry,
and your desire toward Him shall be
generously rewarded.

He knows your need and the depth
of your searching. Only as you fight
discouragement can you make room
for Him to bless you in full measure as
He desires to do.

How can I fight discouragement?

Your Life Is as a Weaving

from Come Away My Beloved

Let the peace of God rule in your hearts.

COLOSSIANS 3:15

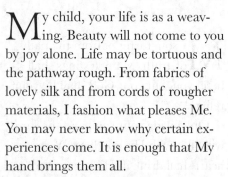

My child, your life is as a weaving. Beauty will not come to you by joy alone. Life may be tortuous and the pathway rough. From fabrics of lovely silk and from cords of rougher materials, I fashion what pleases Me. You may never know why certain experiences come. It is enough that My hand brings them all.

My grace is not limited by sorrow and difficulty. Indeed, it shines like a strand of gold mixed in with the black of grief. My hand moves with infinite love, and I am creating a pattern of intricate beauty.

Never be dismayed. The end will bring rejoicing for both yourself and Me. For you are My workmanship, created in Christ, even in His mind before the worlds existed.

What is God working in my life?

Words of Healing

from *Progress of Another Pilgrim*

Let the word of Christ dwell in you richly in all wisdom; teaching and admonishing one another in psalms and hymns and spiritual songs, singing with grace in your hearts to the Lord.

COLOSSIANS 3:16

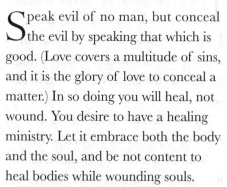

Speak evil of no man, but conceal the evil by speaking that which is good. (Love covers a multitude of sins, and it is the glory of love to conceal a matter.) In so doing you will heal, not wound. You desire to have a healing ministry. Let it embrace both the body and the soul, and be not content to heal bodies while wounding souls.

Learn to minister blessing and comfort to the spirit through your words and thus enhance the ministry of physical healing.

How can I minister blessing and comfort?

November 3

The Bent of the Soul

from *On the Highroad of Surrender*

And whatever you do in word or deed, do all in the
name of the Lord Jesus, giving thanks to God the
Father through Him.

COLOSSIANS 3:17 NKJV

I am in the midst of sorrow and joy alike. I am in business as surely as I am in the sanctuary of worship. In fact, the former becomes the proving ground of the latter. Be content in all places and be at ease in your spirit.

In tests you are made strong. Do not run from them in search of Me.

Your own inner consecration hallows the outer action. Two may do what appears to be the same work. To one it is holy and to the other it is carnal. The difference is in the bent of the soul. . .whether it be for the glory of God or for self-aggrandizement. I breathe My very life into that which is offered to Me as a sacrifice of love.

Do I do all to His glory?

The Prophet's Tongue

from *Make Haste My Beloved*

Let your speech be always with grace, seasoned
with salt, that ye may know how ye ought to
answer every man.

COLOSSIANS 4:6

No prophet of Mine is worthy of the name who brings reproach upon Zion by a careless tongue. He who speaks My words at any time must guard his lips at all times. He is an unworthy mouthpiece who delivers My message in one breath and denies Me in a selfish moment by words that offend My Spirit.

What is my tongue seasoned with?

Praise Transforms

from *On the Highroad of Surrender*

In everything give thanks; for this is the will of
God in Christ Jesus for you.

1 THESSALONIANS 5:18 NKJV

Rejoice in Me always, for as you rejoice and give thanks, you release heaven's treasures and shower upon your head the blessings of a delighted Father. Nothing so thoroughly delights the Father's heart as the praises of His children.

For praise inclines the heart toward gratitude, and gratitude nurtures contentment, and you may know for a certainty that no fruit ever appears on the tree of discontent.

So praise, My children, and never cease in your praising, for in the midst of it I will manifest Myself, and you will understand that when I demand of you your praises, it is for your highest good.

Praise will transform the humblest dwelling to a hallowed haven.

How can I praise God today?

Adversity

from *Progress of Another Pilgrim*

In every thing give thanks: for this is the will of
God in Christ Jesus concerning you.

1 THESSALONIANS 5:18

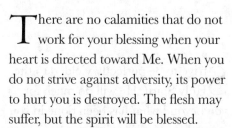

There are no calamities that do not work for your blessing when your heart is directed toward Me. When you do not strive against adversity, its power to hurt you is destroyed. The flesh may suffer, but the spirit will be blessed.

My voice speaks through every situation to the ear that is yielded to the Spirit. My love flows freely through every sorrow to the heart that is devoted to Me. I will not fail anyone—ever, so long as that one is resting and trusting in My goodness.

Evils pass as ships in the night when peace reigns in the surrendered soul. Leave with Me every unsolved problem. Praise Me, and rejoice while I work it all out for My glory.

What unsolved problems can I leave
with the Lord?

I Require More

from *Progress of Another Pilgrim*

And the very God of peace sanctify you wholly;
and I pray God your whole spirit and soul and
body be preserved blameless unto the coming of
our Lord Jesus Christ. Faithful is he that calleth
you, who also will do it.

1 THESSALONIANS 5:23–24

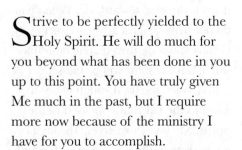

Strive to be perfectly yielded to the Holy Spirit. He will do much for you beyond what has been done in you up to this point. You have truly given Me much in the past, but I require more now because of the ministry I have for you to accomplish.

Let Me work in you with full liberty. You cannot do it yourself. I am the sanctifier. Only give Me the freedom to work. You will be amazed at how easily it can be done.

How much freedom have I given God to work in my life?

Set Your Course by My Promises

from *Come Away My Beloved*

The Lord is faithful, who will establish you and
guard you from the evil one.

2 THESSALONIANS 3:3 NKJV

Be not afraid. I will not allow your adversaries to swallow you up. You are My child; I will deliver you, honor you, and be glorified through you. Because of My faithfulness to you, even your enemies will recognize My power. Hold to My promises. They are given to you as a chart is given to a ship, and a compass to the hunter. You may set your course and find your way by My promises. They will lead you and guide you in places where there is no trodden path.

Study My Word. It abounds with nuggets of courage. It will strengthen you and help you, and even in eternity you will partake of its far-reaching effects.

*How much do God's promises
chart my course?*

Eternal Destiny of the Present Moment

from *Come Away My Beloved*

Be an example to the believers in word, in conduct,
in love, in spirit, in faith, in purity.

1 TIMOTHY 4:12 NKJV

O My child, it is not appointed to you to know the future. It is enough that we should walk together in love and trust. No doubts need mar your peace. Rest in the knowledge that My ways are perfect and My grace is all-sufficient. My help is adequate, no matter what may befall you.

Let no one say to you, "This will be, or that will surely come to pass." Live, rather, in the awareness of the eternal destiny of the present moment. To be unduly occupied with matters of the future is to your own disadvantage. So much is waiting to be done now.

Am I sensing the eternal destiny of the present moment?

Be Not Negligent

from *Progress of Another Pilgrim*

Wherefore I put thee in remembrance that thou
stir up the gift of God, which is in thee by the
putting on of my hands.

2 TIMOTHY 1:6

Be not negligent concerning the
gift I have given you. Do not allow
it to become dormant. I have given it
to you knowing full well the urgency
of this hour. Be up and about your
Father's business. Let nothing else
claim priority over this, My commis-
sion to you.

You shall suffer loss, and not you
alone but multitudes of others, if
indolence overtakes you. My people
are searching for food, and the pastures are sparse. There is need for the
provision of nourishment. Yes, My
Body must be fed and cared for and
supplied the necessary nutriments for
health and growth.

*Am I negligent or industrious about my
Father's business?*

November 11

Eternal Values

from *Progress of Another Pilgrim*

For the which cause I also suffer these things:
nevertheless I am not ashamed: for I know whom
I have believed, and am persuaded that he is
able to keep that which I have committed unto
him against that day.

2 TIMOTHY 1:12

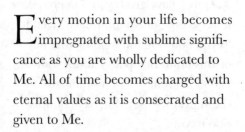

Every motion in your life becomes impregnated with sublime significance as you are wholly dedicated to Me. All of time becomes charged with eternal values as it is consecrated and given to Me.

How dedicated am I to God?

Release the
Blessings Also

from *Progress of Another Pilgrim*

That good thing which was committed unto thee
keep by the Holy Ghost which dwelleth in us.

2 TIMOTHY 1:14

You are accustomed to give Me liberty to take from you all that is displeasing to Me. Now I ask that you give Me daily all that blesses. I will bless it and protect it and safeguard it for you.

All rest of heart comes through committal. You have been taught to release your burdens. Part of your anxiety at this moment has come from a feeling of responsibility to the care of that priceless thing which I Myself have given you. So I say: Give it to Me! I will not *take* it from you, but I will *keep* it for you, and thus it shall be twice blessed.

Let Me guard your treasure.

*What blessings do I need to release
back to God?*

Triumphs Rise Out of Defeats

from *Progress of Another Pilgrim*

If we suffer, we shall also reign with him:
if we deny him, he also will deny us.

2 TIMOTHY 2:12

Be patient as My hand deals with you. Blessings are born out of pain. Triumphs rise out of the dust of defeats when the defeats are offered up to Me and you go on again in faith.

Never despair.

When have I trusted my defeats to God's hand?

Preparation

from *Progress of Another Pilgrim*

Study to shew thyself approved unto God, a
workman that needeth not to be ashamed, rightly
dividing the word of truth.

2 TIMOTHY 2:15

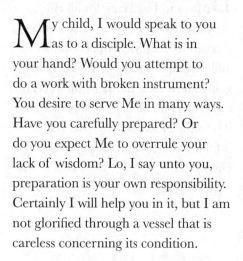

My child, I would speak to you as to a disciple. What is in your hand? Would you attempt to do a work with broken instrument? You desire to serve Me in many ways. Have you carefully prepared? Or do you expect Me to overrule your lack of wisdom? Lo, I say unto you, preparation is your own responsibility. Certainly I will help you in it, but I am not glorified through a vessel that is careless concerning its condition.

How well prepared am I to serve God?

November 15

Useless Striving

from *Make Haste, My Beloved*

The servant of God must not strive.

2 TIMOTHY 2:24

Be careful that you are following Me, and I will care for all else. Striving is for those who have not yet learned to trust Me. Anxiety is the affliction of the self-possessed. The godly know their heritage and revel in the protection of their Redeemer. For it is in the blood of Jesus that refuge is found for every onslaught of the enemy.

What is my spiritual heritage?

A Perpetual Fountain
of Glory

from *Come Away My Beloved*

I have fought the good fight, I have finished the
race, I have kept the faith.

2 TIMOTHY 4:7 NKJV

Write those things I say to you.
Hold back nothing of all I shall
say to you. For I shall speak to you in
the darkness and shall make your way
a path of light. I will cry to you out of
the confusion round about, and you
shall hear My voice and shall know that
which I do.

Look to Me, and I will be your
beacon in the night, and you will not
stumble over the hidden things. You
will walk in a way of victory though
turmoil is on either hand, even as Israel marched through the Red Sea on
a path My hand hewed out for them.

Am I looking only to Jesus?

November 17

Dependence on God

from *Come Away My Beloved*

For we have become partakers of Christ if
we hold the beginning of our confidence
steadfast to the end.
HEBREWS 3:14 NKJV

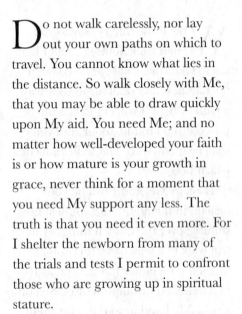

Do not walk carelessly, nor lay
out your own paths on which to
travel. You cannot know what lies in
the distance. So walk closely with Me,
that you may be able to draw quickly
upon My aid. You need Me; and no
matter how well-developed your faith
is or how mature is your growth in
grace, never think for a moment that
you need My support any less. The
truth is that you need it even more. For
I shelter the newborn from many of
the trials and tests I permit to confront
those who are growing up in spiritual
stature.

Move forward with courage and
confidence; but always allow Me to
walk ahead, and choose the right path.

When have I walked behind Jesus?

Discover the Power of Truth

from *Progress of Another Pilgrim*

For the word of God is quick, and powerful, and sharper than any twoedged sword, piercing even to the dividing asunder of soul and spirit, and of the joints and marrow, and is a discerner of the thoughts and intents of the heart.

HEBREWS 4:12

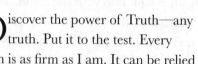

Discover the power of Truth—any truth. Put it to the test. Every truth is as firm as I am. It can be relied upon. It can be trusted as a fact and counted upon in experience.

Believe My truths, but go beyond this. Put them into operation, and learn what it is to experience them as well. Only in this way can you proclaim their fact in a persuasive manner. No teaching is effective except as it springs out of experience, and no teaching which does spring from experience shall fall short.

Which of God's truths do I need to put into operation in my life?

Total Relinquishment

from *Progress of Another Pilgrim*

For we have not an high priest which cannot be
touched with the feeling of our infirmities; but was
in all points tempted like as we are, yet without sin.

HEBREWS 4:15

As you ponder the sufferings of
the Lord Jesus Christ, you shall
gain insight into your own pain. That
which is of the Spirit must be discerned in the Spirit. Only in prayer
and meditation on the Holy Word can
understanding come to your heart,
and only thus can you be truly comforted in the depth of the spirit where
the suffering occurs.

Nothing can remain of self-will if
My full purpose is to be accomplished.
Slowly, unrelentingly, each soul moves
to his own Gethsemane of total relinquishment of all his cherished personal hopes and on to his own barren
Golgotha.

When has my self-will limited God's purpose
in my life?

The Singing Heart

from *On the Highroad of Surrender*

Now faith is the substance of things hoped for, the
evidence of things not seen.

HEBREWS 11:1

Patience, My child, will manifest
where hope is nurtured. The
singing heart is blind to obstacles and
recognizes in all things the loving
hand of an all-wise Father. In such
a state, delays are unnoticed, for the
Spirit is not bound by the limitations
of outer circumstances. The power
of evil to destroy joy is nullified when
Christ Himself becomes the one point
of attention. In Him all things are
possessed now for faith beholds that
which is yet to be as though it were
already a reality.

Withdraw your attention from the
outer circumstance and lose yourself,
My child, in the free-flowing stream of
the Spirit.

*What "outer circumstances" do I need to look
past today?*

Sincerity

from *Come Away My Beloved*

But without faith it is impossible to please Him,
for he who comes to God must believe that
He is, and that He is a rewarder of those who
diligently seek Him.

HEBREWS 11:6 NKJV

———— ⌁ ————

Marvel not that I have said you must be born anew. Of the flesh, nothing spiritual can ever be produced.

This is why I said I loathed your sacrifices. It was not that I despised the ordinance in itself, but I perceived that it was an expression of self-righteousness, showing your indifference to the claim of God upon your heart.

My ordinances are good and holy, but they are to be entered into with deep sincerity and with awareness of their true significance. To sacrifice in carelessness and ignorance is to damage your own soul. Let your spirit never become callous.

What is my heart attitude in sacrifice?

Run with Patience

from *Come Away My Beloved*

Wherefore seeing we also are compassed about
with so great a cloud of witnesses, let us lay aside
every weight, and the sin which doth so easily beset
us, and let us run with patience the race
that is set before us.

HEBREWS 12:1

I could by adversity strip from you
the comforts of life, but I will bless
you in double portion if, of your own
accord, you do as the apostle Paul
and lay aside every weight, resisting
the many temptations that continually
beset you as you run with patience the
course I set before you.

"Running" with "patience"—in
these two words I have combined the
intensity of purpose and the quiet
waiting upon Me you must have, or
else you will be overtaken in the race
by fatigue of body and soul.

*How patiently am I running the race
before me?*

November 23

Hold Fast

from Come Away My Beloved

Looking unto Jesus, the author and finisher of
our faith, who for the joy that was set before Him
endured the cross, despising the shame, and has sat
down at the right hand of the throne of God.

HEBREWS 12:2 NKJV

***

Hold fast that which you have, and
let no one take your crown.
Let no one hinder you in pursuit of the
reward.
Let nothing stand in the way of your
complete victory.
Let no weariness or discouraging
thought cause you to loosen the rope
of faith, but bind it tighter and a
chor fast to My Word.
My Word can never fail.
Emmanuel! God with us!
Praise His holy, wonderful Name! For
this He made us.
For this He destined us! For this He
predestinated us!
For this He died and rose.
For this He sent that first mighty ou
pouring at Pentecost.
Praise God! Praise God!

What stands in the way of my complete victory?

The Art of Constancy

from *Progress of Another Pilgrim*

By him therefore let us offer the sacrifice of praise
to God continually, that is, the fruit of our lips
giving thanks to his name.

HEBREWS 13:15

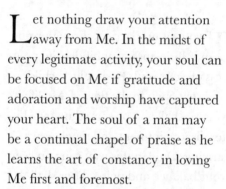

L et nothing draw your attention away from Me. In the midst of every legitimate activity, your soul can be focused on Me if gratitude and adoration and worship have captured your heart. The soul of a man may be a continual chapel of praise as he learns the art of constancy in loving Me first and foremost.

You frequently emphasize how much you should love Me. This is important, but even more important to Me, and to you, is the constancy of your love. . .that it be the overflowing grace of your heart continually, so that every waking hour you are truly and literally walking and worshipping in the Spirit.

How can worship overflow in my life?

Perfecting of Soul

from *Progress of Another Pilgrim*

Now the God of peace. . .make you perfect in
every good work to do his will, working in you that
which is wellpleasing in his sight, through Jesus
Christ; to whom be glory for ever and ever. Amen.

HEBREWS 13:20–21

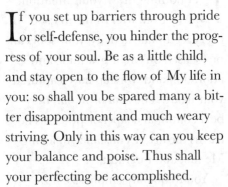

If you set up barriers through pride
or self-defense, you hinder the progress of your soul. Be as a little child,
and stay open to the flow of My life in
you: so shall you be spared many a bitter disappointment and much weary
striving. Only in this way can you keep
your balance and poise. Thus shall
your perfecting be accomplished.

Nothing you could ever do for Me
can be more important than this—the
perfecting of your own soul.

How has pride hindered the progress
of my soul?

Patience and Perfection

from *Progress of Another Pilgrim*

But let patience have her perfect work, that ye may
be perfect and entire, wanting nothing.

JAMES 1:4

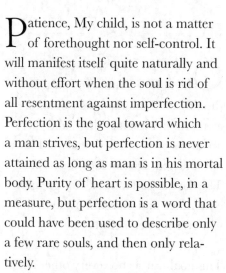

Patience, My child, is not a matter
of forethought nor self-control. It
will manifest itself quite naturally and
without effort when the soul is rid of
all resentment against imperfection.
Perfection is the goal toward which
a man strives, but perfection is never
attained as long as man is in his mortal
body. Purity of heart is possible, in a
measure, but perfection is a word that
could have been used to describe only
a few rare souls, and then only relatively.

The only way you can make any
reasonable progress toward perfection
is by committing your entire life into
My hands and realizing it is I who live
within you and effect whatever changes are made.

Is patience working in my life?

The Need for
Greater Faith

from *Come Away My Beloved*

If any of you lacks wisdom, let him ask of God,
who gives to all liberally and without reproach,
and it will be given to him.

JAMES 1:5 NKJV

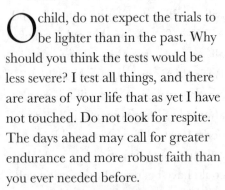

O child, do not expect the trials to be lighter than in the past. Why should you think the tests would be less severe? I test all things, and there are areas of your life that as yet I have not touched. Do not look for respite. The days ahead may call for greater endurance and more robust faith than you ever needed before.

Apply your heart to learn wisdom. This goal transcends every other aim, and any other good that comes out of a pressure period is an added blessing in excess.

Seek Me above all else.

How important to me is wisdom?

Tensions Build Fortitude

from Progress of Another Pilgrim

Blessed is the man that endureth temptation: for
when he is tried, he shall receive the crown of life,
which the Lord hath promised to them
that love him.

JAMES 1:12

Many perplexities bring you closer to Me, for as you seek wisdom and need courage, you are driven to Me for help. These are the times you become pliable in My hands. It is the moment of crisis that reveals either a man's strength or his weakness. It is the tension of life that builds fortitude or exposes fear.

Know that I keep you, that I love you, that I fully understand. Cast yourself wholly upon My mercy. Pray, knowing that the request is already granted and the help already provided.

Act in faith: it is the secret of every victory.

When has tension pushed me nearer to God?

Love and Vain Religion

from *Make Haste My Beloved*

Pure religion and undefiled before God and the
Father is this, To visit the fatherless and widows
in their affliction, and to keep himself unspotted
from the world.

JAMES 1:27

He who does not express love exposes the darkness of his soul, though he be clothed with religion. This man's religion is vain, wrote James, if he does not express his faith by kindness and good deeds (James 1:26–27). He needs no man to condemn him; he condemns himself by his failure to show consideration for the feelings of his brother. No amount of pious platitudes can outweigh his guilt. He has appointed himself to a high place and is scarcely fit for the lowest.

"But he that is greatest among you shall be your servant," said Jesus (Matthew 23:11).

Is my religion vain or pure?

Let Him Take the Initiative

from *Progress of Another Pilgrim*

Submit yourselves therefore to God.

JAMES 4:7

Let no selfish motives rule your actions. Be motivated by the love of God, and if you truly are, you can rest assured that whatever you do has the approval of your Father.

You cannot do with joy some of the things that may be permissible for another. You are not free to make your own choices as long as you are surrendered to the Will of God, for when you are yielded to Him, it is He who gives the directions. Wait for Him to take the initiative.

When have I let God take the initiative in my life?

December 1

Heart-Purity

from *Come Away My Beloved*

Therefore submit to God. Resist the devil and he
will flee from you. Draw near to God and He will
draw near to you.

JAMES 4:7–8 NKJV

My children, it is not by grieving over your sins that they are
forgiven. My forgiveness is in constant
operation and you need only accept it.
The cleansing of your heart and the
restoration of your joy depends upon
your full confession and willingness
to repent and to renounce your sin.
Exercise your soul toward the achievement of heart-purity. Until this work
is accomplished (and maintained) you
will not have inner peace.

This unrest and conflict is not
caused by My attitude toward you but
by your attitude toward yourself. Seek
My face in repentance until you have
yielded to Me all that distresses you.

How do I view my own sins?

I Seek to Lift Your Load

from *Come Away My Beloved*

Humble yourselves in the sight of the Lord,
and He will lift you up.
JAMES 4:10 NKJV

———— ⟨⟩ ————

Seek Me early; seek Me late; seek
Me in the midst of the day. You
need Me in the early hours for direction and guidance and for My blessing
upon your heart. You need Me at the
end of the day to commit into My
hands the day's happenings—both
to free yourself of the burdens and
to give them over into My hands so
I may continue to work things out.
And you need Me more than ever in
the busy hours, so that I may give you
My grace and My tranquility and My
wisdom.

I desire to take the tensions of life
from you.

How humble am I before God?

Conviction and Forgiveness

from *Come Away My Beloved*

Confess your trespasses to one another, and pray for one another, that you may be healed. The effective, fervent prayer of a righteous man avails much.

JAMES 5:16 NKJV

My patience is running out. I have purposed and man has despised. I have willed and you have resisted me. Do not be smug in your own ways; for your ways are not My ways.

You are indulgent when I have called you to rigid discipline. You speak soft words when I would require you to speak the truth. You interfere with the convicting work of My Holy Spirit when you smooth over confession. I am not a severe God, unmindful of the frailties of human nature; but I am a God of divine love and holiness, and I desire your fellowship, and I long for you to know My joy.

What do I need to confess?

Rely on My Faithfulness

from *Progress of Another Pilgrim*

[You] who are kept by the power of God through
faith unto salvation ready to be revealed
in the last time.

1 PETER 1:5

Do not be anxious. My Spirit shall direct your steps. You need have no fear. There is never a place where you walk that I have not preceded you. There are many times when your faith wavers. Take no account of it. I am keeping you even when you do not feel strong. You must rely on My faithfulness—not on your feelings.

Your strength will vary from day to day, but My power is always available to you as you yield to the Holy Spirit.

Do I rely on His faithfulness or my feelings?

December 5

An Injection of
New Life

from *Progress of Another Pilgrim*

Wherein ye greatly rejoice, though now for a
season, if need be, ye are in heaviness through
manifold temptations.

1 PETER 1:6

A ll you do for Me in ministering to others is part of My own working within you; for in every case, whenever you bless another, you bring an injection of new life and vitality into your own spirit and personality.

Your character is that which I shape from the broken fragments of all your testings; therefore, accept the trials with a grateful heart. I will use all things to bring you into conformity to My image if you will but bless all and trust Me.

How complete is my trust in God?

Testings

from *Progress of Another Pilgrim*

That the trial of your faith, being much more precious
than of gold that perisheth, though it be tried with
fire, might be found unto praise and honour and
glory at the appearing of Jesus Christ.

1 PETER 1:7

In a multitude of testings I would
perfect your understanding. I am
not unaware of the pressures thus inflicted upon you, but as the trials come
and go, I not only turn them into a
means of blessing, but I never fail to
make available My comfort and My
sustaining strength.

How has God blessed me through trials?

December 7

The Headship of Christ

from *Progress of Another Pilgrim*

Wherefore gird up the loins of your mind, be sober,
and hope to the end for the grace that is to be
brought unto you at the revelation of Jesus Christ.

1 PETER 1:13

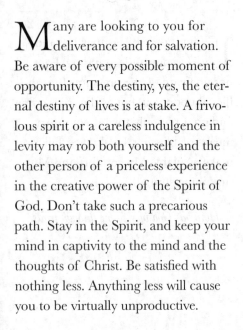

Many are looking to you for deliverance and for salvation. Be aware of every possible moment of opportunity. The destiny, yes, the eternal destiny of lives is at stake. A frivolous spirit or a careless indulgence in levity may rob both yourself and the other person of a priceless experience in the creative power of the Spirit of God. Don't take such a precarious path. Stay in the Spirit, and keep your mind in captivity to the mind and the thoughts of Christ. Be satisfied with nothing less. Anything less will cause you to be virtually unproductive.

*Who might be looking to me for
deliverance?*

God's Mercy

from Come Away My Beloved

And above all things have fervent charity among
yourselves: for charity shall cover the
multitude of sins.

1 PETER 4:8

If it is true that human love covers a
multitude of sins, how much more
true is it of the divine love of God the
Father! Knowing My deep love for
you, your own heart will no longer
condemn you. My mercies are everlasting, My kindness, abundant.

My grace extends to the least of
My children, and My tenderness shall
make you strong. I go before you daily
to prepare your way, and you will be
accompanied by My goodness and My
mercy.

*When have I thanked God for His
goodness and mercy?*

Tribulation

from On the Highroad of Surrender

Beloved, do not think it strange concerning the
fiery trial which is to try you, as though some
strange thing happened to you.

1 PETER 4:12 NKJV

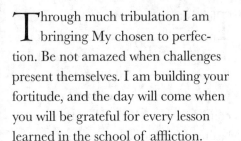

Through much tribulation I am
bringing My chosen to perfection. Be not amazed when challenges
present themselves. I am building your
fortitude, and the day will come when
you will be grateful for every lesson
learned in the school of affliction.

*How grateful am I for God's
lessons in affliction?*

I Shall Gather
My People

from *Come Away My Beloved*

For the time has come for judgment to begin at
the house of God; and if it begins with us first,
what will be the end of those who do not obey the
gospel of God?

1 PETER 4:17 NKJV

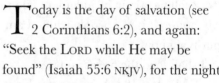

Today is the day of salvation (see
2 Corinthians 6:2), and again:
"Seek the LORD while He may be
found" (Isaiah 55:6 NKJV), for the night
comes. Then My wrath will be poured
out upon the ungodly, and there will
be no hand stretched forth to save.

Lift your eyes to the clouds, for the
heavens are filled with glory. Yes, He
comes with ten thousand of His saints.
Lift your hearts, for you will not be
afraid of those things that are coming to pass upon the earth. For I shall
gather My people to Myself; and the
flames will not touch them.

*How do I feel about "those things that are
coming to pass"?*

A Rain of Fire

from *Make Haste My Beloved*

For the time is come that judgment must begin at
the house of God; and if it first begin at us, what
shall the end be of them that obey not
the gospel of God?

1 PETER 4:17

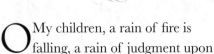

OMy children, a rain of fire is
falling, a rain of judgment upon
My house. It is My people whom I am
purifying now.

I shall send the fire as you wait
upon Me. It shall bring you refreshing
as a rain. It shall be death to the old
carnal nature, but it shall be life to the
inner man—the new nature that is
yours in Christ.

Never be afraid of My judgments.
I do not send them in wrath upon My
church, but in love and compassion.
Can I abandon you to your sin?

*Can I see God's compassion in His
judgments?*

As Rains of Refreshing

from *Come Away My Beloved*

Humble yourselves therefore under the mighty
hand of God, that he may exalt you in due time.

1 PETER 5:6

———— ❧ ————

O My beloved, do not be anxious
concerning tomorrow. You shall
encounter nothing of which I am not
already aware. My mercy is concealed
within every storm cloud. My grace
flows beneath every crosscurrent. My
wisdom has conceived a solution to
every perplexity.

I have deliberately set obstacles in
your path to test your prowess. The
storm is not a thing to fear but rather
to welcome. As soon as you have made
the discovery that in the time of stress
and strain you have the clearest revelations of Myself, You will learn to head
into the wind with sheer delight.

How do I view spiritual obstacles?

December 13

A Covert in the Storm

from On the Highroad of Surrender

Therefore humble yourselves under the mighty
hand of God, that He may exalt you in due time,
casting all your care upon Him,
for He cares for you.

1 PETER 5:6–7 NKJV

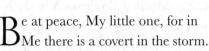

Be at peace, My little one, for in Me there is a covert in the storm. My love remains changeless whatever winds may blow. My grace will sustain you however deep may be the night, however fierce may be the test.

Nothing harms the trusting soul though calamity be his companion. In affliction there shall be comfort, for he who abides in Me shall not know desolation. I protect, I provide, I enrich. None shall say in My presence, "I am poor," for he who loves Me is supremely blessed; My grace is his strength, and I am his salvation.

*When have I found God's comfort
in affliction?*

Sincerity

from *Progress of Another Pilgrim*

Be sober, be vigilant; because your adversary the
devil, as a roaring lion, walketh about, seeking
whom he may devour.

1 PETER 5:8

O My child, be truly as a little
child, and preserve within your
spirit the grace of simplicity. Maintain
a candid honesty. Resist all temptation to put on airs. Be natural. Strive
to be as Jesus, who was never pretentious, never evasive nor coy. Be real,
be sincere, for to serve God demands
sincerity. The needs of hearts and
problems of life are real. Many carry
burdens and griefs, and how can you
be of help in a frivolous state of mind?

How sincere is my witness?

December 15

As a Lamb Before a Lion

from *Progress of Another Pilgrim*

Be sober, be vigilant; because your adversary the
devil, as a roaring lion, walketh about, seeking
whom he may devour.

1 PETER 5:8

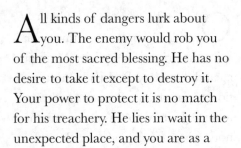

All kinds of dangers lurk about you. The enemy would rob you of the most sacred blessing. He has no desire to take it except to destroy it. Your power to protect it is no match for his treachery. He lies in wait in the unexpected place, and you are as a lamb before a lion.

At My feet leave all, and know it is for your ultimate joy. Truly it is not a sacrifice. It will be your salvation.

What blessing have I left at God's feet?

Crisis Experiences

from *Progress of Another Pilgrim*

But the God of all grace, who hath called us unto
his eternal glory by Christ Jesus, after that ye
have suffered a while, make you perfect, stablish,
strengthen, settle you.

1 PETER 5:10

I will never leave you alone in the
midst of any affliction. You cannot
escape the crisis experiences if you
desire to grow and mature, but you
need never fear them regardless of the
form they take, for My grace and My
equanimity shall be as a strong anchor
that shall hold you fast, and you shall
not be driven off course.

*When have I felt the tug of God's
protecting anchor?*

December 17

Repentance Activates
My Grace

from *Progress of Another Pilgrim*

If we confess our sins, he is faithful and just to
forgive us our sins, and to cleanse us from all
unrighteousness. If we say that we have not sinned,
we make him a liar, and his word is not in us.

1 JOHN 1:9–10

Give Me all: your body, mind, and spirit. Hold nothing back for yourself. Speak to Me often and much. The more you do so, the more I can help you. Full confession brings full forgiveness. True humility opens the door to divine aid. Genuine repentance activates My grace.

What sins do I need to confess to God?

Fresh Anointing

from *Dialogues with God*

And the world passeth away, and the lust thereof:
but he that doeth the will of God abideth for ever.

1 JOHN 2:17

This is the doing of the will of
God.

As it is written,

He that doeth the will of God abideth
for ever. Service to Me by the
will of the flesh is temporal, but
the doing of the will of God is eternal.

And this is the will of God, that ye be
about the Father's business—that ye
work the works of Him that hath
called thee and now sends thee,
even as did Jesus when He walked
among men.

Leave all else to Me.

Seek the fresh anointing and I will do
the rest.

What is God's will for me today?

Not Lethargy but Surrender

from *Progress of Another Pilgrim*

And the world passeth away, and the lust thereof:
but he that doeth the will of God abideth for ever.

1 JOHN 2:17

You are called not to lethargy but surrender.

Happy is the man who puts his trust in the Lord, yes, even to the extent that he lets Him formulate the plans and direct the goings.

No reward is sweeter than to feel His commendation. No life is more tranquil than that lived in His will. At His feet there is peace. Turmoil shall not dwell in the home where Christ is the honored guest.

All of life becomes a hymn of praise when God's love rules the heart.

Is my life a hymn of praise?

Be Not Afraid of Solitude

from *Progress of Another Pilgrim*

But the anointing which ye have received of him abideth in you, and ye need not that any man teach you: but as the same anointing teacheth you of all things, and is truth, and is no lie, and even as it hath taught you, ye shall abide in him.

1 JOHN 2:27

I have a ministry for you. You have not found it yet because you have been earnestly and in sincerity and with humble heart trying to conform to the patterns of others.

Be not afraid of solitude. You will not lose My touch. You will not miss a blessing. How shall the hand of any other bring you greater joy or clearer insight than I can bring to you Myself?

Is there a ministry I need to seek His will on?

December 21

My Love Is Coexistent with My Power

from Dialogues with God

God is love; and he that dwelleth in love
dwelleth in God.

1 John 4:16

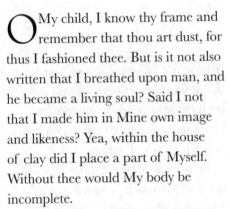

O My child, I know thy frame and remember that thou art dust, for thus I fashioned thee. But is it not also written that I breathed upon man, and he became a living soul? Said I not that I made him in Mine own image and likeness? Yea, within the house of clay did I place a part of Myself. Without thee would My body be incomplete.

Draw near to My heart; for My love for thee is coexistent with My power. Yea, e'er thy face touch the dust, I have put Mine arms about thee to draw thee unto My heart.

When have I drawn near to His heart?

Identity

from *On the Highroad of Surrender*

We love Him because He first loved us. If someone
says, "I love God," and hates his brother, he is a
liar; for he who does not love his brother whom he has
seen, how can he love God whom he has not seen?

1 JOHN 4:19–20 NKJV

Out of much tribulation I bring
forth a people for the glory of
My Name. I am shaping you in the
furnace of affliction that I may set My
seal upon you and display in you My
own identity. I desire that you be one
with Me in all I have purposed.

My heart is grieved when those
who profess to be My children neglect
their intercessory prayer life. They do
damage to the spirit of grace when
they neglect their responsibility toward
others. Can you love God while ignoring the need of your brother?

Whom should I pray for today?

December 23

Physical Health and Spiritual Ministry

from *Progress of Another Pilgrim*

Beloved, I wish above all things that thou mayest
prosper and be in health, even as thy soul prospereth.

3 JOHN 1:2

Do not misconstrue the scripture
which says "I beat my body to
keep it in subjection." A more clear
way to state the true intent would be
to say, "By proper discipline and care
of the physical body, it may be made
to fulfill the desires and demands of
the soul." Otherwise, you may, by lack
of concern for your physical health,
hamper your spiritual ministry.

Run the race with a pure heart, and
the reward shall be given you. Your
path is strewn with blessings. Enjoy
them fully and recognize that they are
from My hand.

*How do I discipline and care for
my body?*

Praying in the Spirit

from *Come Away My Beloved*

But you, beloved, building yourselves up on your
most holy faith, praying in the Holy Spirit, keep
yourselves in the love of God.

JUDE 20–21 NKJV

As you set your soul through deliberate choice of your will to worship Me by praying in the Spirit, you will find your faith strengthened and your life bathed in My love.

With your faith laying hold on My promises and power, and your actions motivated by My love, you will find yourself in the path of My activity; My blessing shall be upon you, and I will accomplish My works through you.

Am I praying in the Spirit?

December 25

Vital Contact

from *Progress of Another Pilgrim*

But ye, beloved, building up yourselves on your
most holy faith, praying in the Holy Ghost, keep
yourselves in the love of God, looking for the
mercy of our Lord Jesus Christ unto eternal life.

JUDE 20–21

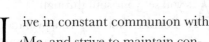

Live in constant communion with
Me, and strive to maintain continual vital contact. So shall be generated within you the spiritual power
which builds up a ready supply for the
moments of actual ministry.

This is the reason Jesus spent long
hours in lonely vigil with His Father.
This is why the scriptures admonish
you to pray without ceasing.

As you pray and meditate, you are
enriched by the Spirit in the grace and
compassion of Jesus Christ. Your soul
is perfected as you kneel in His presence, even as a flower unfolds in the
sunshine.

When can I make time for contact with God?

The Last Great Outpouring

from *Come Away My Beloved*

"I am the Alpha and the Omega, the Beginning and the End," says the Lord, "who is and who was and who is to come, the Almighty."
REVELATION 1:8 NKJV

—————— ∼ ——————

You stand on the threshold of a new day. I have truly great things in store for you. I will bring to pass a new thing. You have heard of the showers, but I say to you: I will send a mighty downpour. In the day of the great deluge which is coming, many will come to know the reality of My power.

Surely I will pour out My Spirit, I will reaffirm the veracity of My Word and bring the message of the Gospel of Redemption to many who would otherwise never give heed. I am the Alpha and the Omega. Stand firm in Me. Never waver.

Am I standing firm, without wavering?

Warring in the Spirit

from On the Highroad of Surrender

And they overcame him by the blood of the Lamb
and by the word of their testimony, and they did
not love their lives to the death.

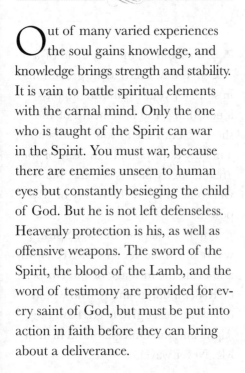

Out of many varied experiences the soul gains knowledge, and knowledge brings strength and stability. It is vain to battle spiritual elements with the carnal mind. Only the one who is taught of the Spirit can war in the Spirit. You must war, because there are enemies unseen to human eyes but constantly besieging the child of God. But he is not left defenseless. Heavenly protection is his, as well as offensive weapons. The sword of the Spirit, the blood of the Lamb, and the word of testimony are provided for every saint of God, but must be put into action in faith before they can bring about a deliverance.

How can I prepare for spiritual warfare?

My Kingdom Is at Hand

from Come Away My Beloved

Fear God and give glory to Him, for the hour of
His judgment has come; and worship Him who
made heaven and earth, the sea and springs
of water.

By My Spirit, I will speak to My
people. Those who hear My voice
will sing of My glory. Those who are
pure of heart will walk in a path of
delight. Joy is the natural climate of
heaven, and My chosen ones will have
a full portion even now.

Be prepared for Me, for I will come
to you in blinding splendor, and you
will not be able to bear it if you have
been regarding the darkness about
you. Look above the present scene, for
to dwell on the confusion of the world
would render you unfit for the revelation of heaven.

How prepared am I for the Lord's return?

December 29

Prepare Your Garments

from Progress of Another Pilgrim

And to her was granted that she should be arrayed
in fine linen, clean and white: for the fine linen is
the righteousness of saints.

REVELATION 19:8

———— ∼ ————

The day is at hand, and the Day Star riseth even now. You may not see Me yet, but I am only just beneath the rim of the horizon, and you shall behold Me shortly in all My glory.

How ought you to rise and make yourself ready! How you should put your house in order and prepare your garments!

Your garments shall be of fine linen, for it is the righteousness of the saints.

What can I do to prepare my garments?

Vivid Relationship

from *Dialogues with God*

Out of his mouth goeth a sharp sword, that with it
he should smite the nations: and he shall rule them
with a rod of iron: and he treadeth the winepress of
the fierceness and wrath of Almighty God.

REVELATION 19:15

Wonderful Saviour! Blessed, holy
sacrificial Lamb of God! What
depth of love Thou hast demonstrated
for us through Thy vicarious death
on Calvary; and in Thy resurrection,
what sublime victory! What dynamic
power was revealed in Thine ascen-
sion, what promise of life to come, of
ultimate triumph, of complete deliverance from this present world, from
suffering and shame—sin and death.

Lo, what great hope is set before us!
Yea, what glory; what rapture—what
a mighty deliverance—what victory!
Let Satan do his worst: Christ has
overcome.

What trials in my life can Christ
overcome?

December 31

No Separation

from *Come Away My Beloved*

And I saw a new heaven and a new earth: for the
first heaven and the first earth were passed away;
and there was no more sea.

REVELATION 21:1

He has stretched forth His mighty
hand
And has smitten the waters:
He has made me to pass through dry-
shod. Hallelujah! For there will be
no more sea.
There will be no more separation!
He has removed every barrier; He has
bridged the gulf. He has drawn me
unto Himself, yes, into Himself.
He has left the enemy in confusion
and defeat.
He has led me through the way of the
wilderness,
And His hand has been a shade from
the burning heat.

When have I praised God for these blessings?

SCRIPTURE INDEX

OLD TESTAMENT

NEW TESTAMENT